THE STOR
STAMFORD HOSPITAL

As told in the 19th, 20th and 21st centuries

The Friends of Stamford Hospital

)

Published by the Friends of Stamford Hospital
Printed by Spiegl Press Ltd. Stamford
ISBN 978-1-5262-0404-2

CONTENTS

Introduction

History of Stamford, Rutland and general infirmary: 1879

A Short History of the Stamford and Rutland Hospital: 1978

The continuing story - 1978 to 2015

INTRODUCTION

Two previous histories of Stamford Hospital exist. The first was entitled "History of Stamford, Rutland and General Infirmary" written by William Newman, a Surgeon at the Hospital, and was printed in 1879. The second was entitled "A Short History of the Stamford and Rutland Hospital" and was commissioned in 1978 by the Friends of Stamford Hospital to mark the 150th anniversary of the Hospital's foundation.

Both histories were printed and widely circulated, but neither was published as a book, and there is a risk that they might get lost in the future. Recognizing the importance of these documents, and the interest there is in the Hospital's history, the committee of the Friends of Stamford Hospital agreed to publish them unchanged in a new book, and to add a further brief history covering the years 1978 to 2015.

The histories are presented in chronological order and the two earlier accounts are facsimiles of the originals.

Michael Dronfield, Chairman of Friends. Nov. 2015

DR WILLIAM NEWMAN'S HISTORY OF THE STAMFORD, RUTLAND AND GENERAL INFIRMARY: 1879

Dr Newman was a Hospital Surgeon, General Practitioner, author of two editions of the History of Stamford Hospital and also a fine photographer for illustrations in his books. His campaign to improve the hospital resulted in major additions, for example the new Sanitary Blocks and the Fever Blocks.

HISTORY

OF THE

STAMFORD, RUTLAND, & GENERAL INFIRMARY.

—————◆—————

ESTABLISHED IN 1828.

—————◆—————

" Medicus curat, Natura sanat, morbos."

—————

WILLIAM NEWMAN, M.D. Lond. F.R.C,S. Eng. (Exam.)

One of the Surgeons to the Stamford Infirmary.

—————

JENKINSON AND SONS, MACHINE PRINTERS, 58, HIGH STREET.

—

1879.

IT has seemed desirable that some such record, as that which the present pages are intended to convey, should be made of the past history and present conditions of the Stamford Infirmary.

For more than fifty years the daily beneficent work of the Institution has been going on under the direction of many and various officials, to the great advantage of the community. The founders, with hardly a single exception, have passed away; it were surely worth while to shew how their early purpose has flourished into a permanent existence for good, and to mark the various stages of the career of an establishment, with which so many honoured names in and around Stamford, have been associated.

But more than this may be advanced, for, since buildings even, have a personal history, and speak in no uncertain tones to those who interrogate them, it may well be, that the teachings of this very erection, may, in the slow review of years, and of many earnest efforts for the welfare of the inmates, prove of definite value from more than one point of view.

The records of the Hospital have been carefully examined for the facts of the following notice, and the writer is glad to acknowledge the courtesy of the Committee, in placing the requisite materials so fully at his disposal.

AMONG the well known Monastic Foundations in the Midland Counties, place must certainly be given to the Monastery of the Carmelites or Whitefriars at Stamford. Founded probably before the death of Henry III, in 1272 ; it is said to have been remarkable for the magnificence of its structure,

"And in particular famous for its beautiful Church and Spire, which "last, they say, was very like that fine Spire now belonging to All "Saints' Church, in the Mercat Place, at Stamford."*

This Monastery appears to have been the usual resting-place of the English Monarchs in their journeys to and from the North, Edward III. holding a council here during his stay : and the fraternity, among whom several of the most learned men of the age were to be reckoned, stood high in general estimation, not merely from royal favour, but from the reputation and acquirements of its members. The Monastery was surrendered October 8, 1539.

It has been supposed that the gateway still existing was built by Edward III. and the existence of the royal escutcheon, which may yet be faintly traced on the centre shield, two other lateral shields having lost all traces of ornament, lends some support to this impression.

In the earlier years of the present century, the gateway, in very fair condition, and the walls of the enclosure alone remained to shew something of the past glories of the Carmelite foundation.

In 1823, Mr. Henry Fryer, a well known Surgeon, died in St. Martin's, Stamford : leaving the residue of his personal estate, £7477, to be appropriated to the purposes of an Infirmary—

"On the condition, that, within five years after my death, a General "Infirmary shall be established in the town of Stamford, or in the County "of Rutland."

* Peck, Annals of Stanford, LIB. VIII. par. xxxii.

In 1825, July 2, a public meeting was held in the Town Hall to consider the whole matter. The erection of an Infirmary, to accommodate not more than 20 in-patients, was decided on, and a Committee was appointed to obtain subscriptions and to arrange the necessary details.

On this Committee eighteen gentlemen were nominated ;

The Marquis of Exeter,
Sir John Trollope, Bart.,
Gen. Birch Reynardson,
Dr. Willis,
Thomas Hotchkin, Esq.,
Stafford O'Brien, Esq.,
Gilbert Heathcote, Esq.,
Rev. William Baker,
Rev. K. Foster,

Rev. T. K. Bonney,
Rev. Wm. Hardyman,
Rev. Chas. Swann,
Francis Simpson, Esq.,
James Torkington, Esq.,
Thomas Mills, Esq.,
Benjamin Cooper, Esq.,
Dr. Arnold,
Dr. Hopkinson.

At the next Meeting, July 20, the following names were added to the Committee :

The Earl of Winchilsea and Nottingham,
The Earl Brownlow,
Sir Gilbert Heathcote, Bart. M.P.
Sir Gerard Noel, Bart., M.P.,
Rev. Thos. Roberts,
Rev. Christ. Cookson,

Rev. John Jackson Serocold,
Thos. Hippisley Jackson, Esq.
William Stevenson, Esq.,
Nich. Clarke Stevenson, Esq.
Col. Pierrepont,
John Eagleton, Esq.,
Rev. Robert Boon.

At the meeting of Sept. 13, the following name was added :
Samuel Richard Fydell, Esq.

July 20. A plan was asked from certain Architects—

" For a Building to contain not less than 20 Patients, and to be capable " of conveniently accommodating 32, if necessary."

Sept. 13. It was resolved—

" That the Close, called the White Friars, in Stamford, is the most eligible " site for the erection of the intended Infirmary : and further, that two " plans, viz.—those of Mr. Ireland and Mr. Gandy, be recommended for " adoption."

Sept. 24. At the next meeting, the plan proposed by Mr. Gandy was decided on, and a Committee was appointed to superintend the building of the new Infirmary ; this Committee to consist of :

Marquis of Exeter,   Dr. Arnold,
G. Finch, Esq.,   Dr. Hopkinson.
G. Heathcote, Esq.,

The conveyance of the site of the Infirmary and grounds, by Brownlow, Marquis of Exeter, was dated 11 Oct., 1827, and was enrolled in Chancery 3 Nov., 1828.

The necessary land, upwards of 2 acres, was kindly transferred by Lord Exeter to the Committee at a price much below its estimated value. The contract for building was taken by Mr. Crowe, the conditions being that the foundations be built of Stamford stone laid in Stamford lime, but that the exterior walls be built of Wittering or Barnack Pendel, all quoins, heads, sills, and jambs to be of Ketton stone.

The building as first erected was two stories high, and in its ground plan was oblong in form, with a frontage of 130 feet. If the reader will think of this outline as divided from before backwards by imaginary lines into five equal sections, it will be sufficiently easy to understand the internal arrangements. The centre or *middle* fifth was occupied then as now, by the entrance hall and staircase, with operating room over the hall, on the first floor; in direct line behind these rooms ran the board-room and domestic offices, kitchen, &c. The *outer* fifth contained on each side on the ground floor a ward holding six beds, access being given by a well-lighted passage running from the central hall at the back of the building parallel to its greater length. The upper portion of this division and the *remaining* fifth of the whole space were in the first instance devoted to the requirements of the household.

The Subscribers to the Infirmary met for the first time in a General Meeting on April 26, 1827,—The Marquis of Exeter in the chair—and adopted Rules for the future working of the Institution. The meeting was adjourned until July 21, 1827, and on that occasion two Physicians and a Consulting Surgeon were appointed.

A Subsequent Meeting of the Subscribers was held on Oct. 11, 1827, and then a detailed report was made of the amount subscribed, the totals being :

Donations from all Sources £6108 3 3
Annual Subscriptions... ... ... 386 11 0

The Medical Staff of the Infirmary was made complete by the election of five Surgeons and a resident Apothecary.

The Matron and Porter were chosen at the same meeting.

The Clergymen living in and near Stamford, in some number gave in their names, as willing to help in giving spiritual attention and in reading prayers to the in-patients, and a rotation list for such attendance was drawn up.

1827. Nov. 14. It is stated in the minutes that the sum expended in the erection of the building had been £5793 . 12 . 1. Further amounts however were needed for the providing of certain internal fittings, and for the furnishing of the wards.

1828. In March, a Bazaar was held in Stamford in aid of the funds of the Infirmary, and the large amount of £1768 . 6 . 9, was so obtained ; the following Ladies held stalls :

The Marchioness of Exeter,	Miss Hurst,
Hon. Mrs. Heathcote,	Miss Barnes,
Lady Mary Fludyer,	Miss Booth,
Mrs. O'Brien,	Mrs. Wingfield,
The Countess of Lindsey,	Miss Atlay,
Lady Sophia Whichcote,	Miss Brown,
Miss Arnold,	Miss Torkington,
Mrs. Brereton,	Miss Allix.

The Building was opened for the reception of patients on August 5, 1828.

Twelve in-patients appear to have been provided for.

1828. April 29. A Wash-house and Laundry were found necessary and Contracts were entered into for their erection at a cost of £285.

July 29. A Statement of Accounts was handed to the Committee thus :—

Donations—Total Amount to this date £8612 12 0

Annual Subscriptions 428 16 0

1829. Jan. 6. At the General Meeting a Committee for General purposes was appointed, and Rules for the Management of the Institution were decided on.

March 10. A donation of £1400 was given from the fund of the Rutland Yeomanry.

July 25. It was notified that the Trustees of the late Mr. Henry Fryer, the conditions of that gentleman's will having been complied with, had paid over the legacy to the Trustees of the Infirmary.

1830. Jan. 5. A donation of £325 from the Fund of the Ness Yeomanry was paid to the Committee.

In January, 1831, a donation of £10 was directed to be given to the Medical Book Society from the Funds of the Infirmary for the purchase of Books to be the property of this Institution. This annual payment, continued to the present time by the liberality of successive annual Meetings, and supplemented by the subscriptions of the members, has rendered the existing Medical Library of the Infirmary one of no ordinary value.

1832. July 21. It was decided at a General Meeting that "The disease called Cholera Morbus being now prevalent in the neighbour-"hood of this Hospital, and as some cases may probably be presented for "admission, it be resolved that no person affected with that dreadful "disease, or with any other of an infectious nature, shall be admitted "an in-patient of this Infirmary."

1835. Jan. 13. At the Annual Meeting it was proposed to elect a Chaplain, but the motion was negatived.

1836. Aug. 30. A casual entry in the minutes shews that eighteen in-patients were considered the full number, for whom accommodation could be found in the Building.

1840. Jan. 14. The appointment of Chaplain to this Institution was again considered, and it was resolved that the appointment be for the present deferred.

A very handsome present of valuable Medical Books was made by Dr. Arnold to the Medical Book Society.

1842. Feb. 22. It was decided at a General Meeting of the Governors to add to the building, and enlarge the existing kitchen at an estimated cost of about £300, according to plan submitted by Mr. Browning, the Architect.

1843. July 8. New Rules and Regulations for the better management of the Infirmary were adopted.

1847. Jan. 12. It was notified to the Governors that by the will of Stephen Rowles, Esq., late of Stilton, in the County of Huntingdon, the bulk of his property was bequeathed for the benefit of the Infirmary. Some difficulties arose, and after a time a Suit in Chancery was instituted against the Executors under the Will, and was brought to a close in May, 1849, when the sum of £11,285 1s. 9d., Consols, was directed to be paid over to the Trustees of the Infirmary upon certain conditions as to the disposal of the dividends, which are recorded upon a tablet placed in the entrance hall.

1849. Jan. 9. A legacy of £200 having been left by the late Mrs. Hodson, of Stamford, towards erecting a lodge for the purpose of ensuring the security and privacy of the grounds of the Infirmary—plans for the same were accepted from Mr. Clutton, and tenders for the work were advertised for.

At this meeting it was decided that, in place of the two General Meetings of the Governors, held in January, and July respectively in each year since the establishment of the Institution, one annual meeting only be held in the month of January in each year.

Feb. 13. The tender of Messrs. Thompson and Ruddle, of Peterborough, to build the Porter's Lodge for £367 was accepted.

The lodge, as so constructed, now stands at the entrance to the Infirmary grounds ; the Architect having utilized the front of the old Whitefriars' gateway without change, and having erected behind it a convenient porter's lodge.

October 2. The appointment of a Chaplain to the Infirmary having become imperative under the Lord Chancellor's decree upon Mr. Rowles' will, a General Meeting of the Governors was called for such election.

Three gentlemen were nominated :—

Rev. Denis Edward Jones, B.A.,
Rev. Edward Holmes, B.A.,
Rev. Edward May, M.A.,

and of these the Rev. Denis Edward Jones was elected.

At the same meeting a well merited vote of thanks was given to those Clergymen who had, from the first opening of the Institution, given their services in rotation to the great comfort of the patients.

1852. March 30. The enlargement of the wash-house and adjoining buildings was declared to be desirable, and was consequently decided upon—the cost to be £195.

1858. March 18. It was decided to subscribe ten guineas annually to the Royal Sea Bathing Infirmary, Margate. This subscription was discontinued two or three years subsequently.

1860. Aug. 13. A report was sent in by the Medical Officers urging the desirability of erecting some hot and cold baths for the use of the patients : and showing that a special building for such purposes might be placed at the north-west of the Infirmary.

1861. Jan. 22. In pursuance of the above recommendation a plan was prepared by Mr. Browning, which provided for the erection of a bath room on each side of the building, of a new

Surgery, and a matron's room on the ground floor, for the enlargement of the Board Room, and for the increase in size of the middle wards on the first floor, with other consequent changes. The estimated cost was £730. The suggestions were adopted.

The Baths, with all necessary fittings, were supplied by contract at £140 12s. 6d.

The number of in-patients for whom accommodation was provided was forty four.

1863. Jan. 13. At the Annual Meeting, held this day, the Rules for the management of the Infirmary, which had undergone revision and alteration at the hands of the Managing Committee, were adopted.

1865. Jan. The number of in-patients was reduced to forty two.

1866. July 14. A Report was sent in to the Managing Committee, by the Medical Staff, with reference to the Sanitary condition of the Infirmary, which was considered and adopted.

The number of in-patients was reduced to thirty six.

1867. March 26. It was decided to introduce Gas into the Infirmary.

1871. Jan. 9. An important alteration was made in the mode of electing the House Surgeon : hitherto it had been the custom to elect that Officer by the Governors present at a special meeting convened for that purpose, but it was now decided—

" To vest the election in a Committee to be composed of the Managing "Committee, the Physicians and Surgeons of the Infirmary, and those "Governors who are or have been in the Medical Profession ; such "Committee to have full power to make from time to time such " arrangements as they may think fit."

1872. March 19. Following the example of many towns throughout the kingdom, where Hospitals are in existence, it was decided to establish a Hospital Sunday, and—

"To appeal to the Parochial Clergy and other Ministers of Religion "residing within the area, benefited by the Stamford and Rutland "Infirmary, asking them to preach Sermons annually, in aid of the funds "of this Institution, and to recommend that such Sermons be preached "on the day appointed, as Hospital Sunday for collections in behalf of the "Lincoln County Hospital." (2nd Sunday in October.)

The sums collected in pursuance of this request at the respective Churches and Chapels up to the present time are as follows :—

£	s.	d.		£	s.	d.
1872—197	0	1		1875—247	0	7
1873—251	1	9		1876—211	4	0
1874—264	10	5		1877—170	10	0

It may not be out of place to urge strongly that the very essence of a successful Hospital Sunday consists in the appeal being absolutely simultaneous throughout the given district, so that all those who go to a place of Worship on the day selected, may have the claims of the local Infirmary brought before them by their respective Ministers : the correctness of this view is abundantly borne out by the experience of the Metropolis and other districts, a combined, unanimous, unbroken effort having much more effect than a number of isolated appeals, unconnected with each other, and variable in point of time. Further, the opportunity of giving something to the Institution, in which they or their friends have a very direct interest, is eagerly* embraced by, and should be afforded to the poorer section of the congregations, who are unable to make definite subscriptions, but may readily make some small contributions once in the year.

1873. Feb. 3. It was decided, in accordance with a plan produced by Mr. Browning, to improve the means of access to the end wards on the upper floor. Hitherto, the corridor, in no part of its extent more than three feet wide, had had an inconvenient angle at each extremity, and at its commencement an

---

* On one occasion, to the writer's knowledge, 5 florins were collected from a single pew of apparently quite poor people.

unnecessary door. It was decided to remove the door, to round off the main wall at the corner, and to place the door opening into the ward, in a direct line with the corridor itself.

1875. Feb. 18. A report was read from the Medical Officers directing attention to the need for better ventilation in the wards. It was agreed to to make the changes suggested.

Towards the middle of this year, notice was given to the committee, that a considerable amount had been bequeathed to the Infirmary by the late Mr. Arthur Clay, Surgeon, a member of an old Stamford family, who had recently died in Japan ; and in pursuance of this announcement, the sum of £3552 . 4 . 1, was duly paid over in the following spring.

1876. Jan. 18. It was decided to set apart the sum of £100, annually, to be equally divided among the Medical Staff ; and also to provide a book, in which every Medical Officer shall record his attendance at the Infirmary.

On the same day, a Special Committee was appointed consisting of the following gentlemen, viz. :—

The Marquis of Exeter,
J. H. L. Wingfield, Esq.,
Joseph Phillips, Esq.,
J. Paradise, Esq.,
Geo. Cayley, Esq.,

H. Michelson, Esq.,
W. D. Eddowes, Esq.,
J. M. Heward, Esq.,
Dr. Newman,
Dr. Robbs.

"To consider the best means of providing accommodation for persons "suffering from fever and other infectious diseases ; and

"To propose conditions on which persons who are not objects of "charity, may be admitted to the benefits of the Infirmary, on paying for "their maintenance and medical attendance."

The Committee, to which had been further added—

A. C. Johnson, Esq.,
Lord Kesteven,
Rev. J. Birch Reynardson,

met on several occasions, and ultimately reported to an adjourned General Meeting, held

1876. April 11. It was then decided—

"That the Infirmary be extended for the reception of Patients suffer-
"ing from infectious diseases, with the exception of those excluded by Rule
"51." This rule *absolutely* excludes cases of smallpox.

It was also decided—

"That the Managing Committee be empowered to admit patients,
"above the class of those at present admitted, on such conditions as to
"payment for maintenance and medical attendance, as the Committee,
"having regard to the circumstances of each particular case, may think
"fit to impose."

At subsequent meetings it was resolved to apply to the
Marquis of Exeter, offering to purchase the grass field, east of
the present Infirmary, for the erection of the new buildings.

The subject was brought fully before the Governors at their
Annual Meeting, on

1877, Jan. 16, and the report of the Special Committee
was adopted.

The material part of the report ran as follows :

"Your Committee have carefully considered the question of the extent
"of the proposed addition to the Infirmary, and they are of opinion that
"such addition should be capable of accommodating thirty patients."

"Your Committee recommend that this accommodation should be
"provided in three separate blocks of building, each to contain ten beds,
"and they think that one of such blocks will be in frequent use for the
"reception of cases now admitted to the Infirmary, but which, for many
"reasons, it is found desirable to exclude from the general wards."

"Your Committee instructed Mr. Browning to prepare a design for the
"proposed new buildings, and they have gone over all details most carefully
"with him." "Mr. Browning estimates that the cost, including all internal
"fittings, boundary walls, roads, architect's commission, and furnishing,
"will amount to £7,025."

The land required, valued at £540, was shortly afterwards
transferred to the Governors, and Lord Exeter most kindly gave
the amount of the purchase money as a donation to the building

fund. The conveyance of the site is dated April, 1877, and was enrolled in Chancery in May, 1877. This transfer has vested in the Governors of the Stamford Infirmary the whole enclosure within which the Whitefriars' Monastery formerly stood.

The same Committee was continued in office as a special Building Committee, meeting regularly once in each month, and supervising the works which have been carried on during the past eighteen months by Mr. Thompson, contractor, of Peterborough, under the direct superintendence of Mr. Browning.

A detailed description of these new buildings, now

1879, Jan. practically completed, and shortly to be opened for the reception of patients, will be found at p. 30.

It has seemed best to devote some little separate space to the consideration of the sanitary arrangements; the notices, as they are found in the various books of the Infirmary, are therefore given in order of time.

1827. Sept. 18. A Committee notice contains the acceptance of the architect's plan for four water closets, &c., at an estimated cost of £270. No evidence exists as to the mode in which the refuse was disposed of.

1829. Oct. 13. An inquiry is ordered, in order to devise some means for preventing the unpleasantness which the closets are found to produce, and the report given is as follows—

"That the principal drain had not sufficient fall, and that a cesspool "should be formed near to the closets at each end of the House."

These receptacles were accordingly made, the one at the east end opening directly into the loose oolitic rock, that at the west end being made in a different sub-soil, and therefore needing a brick-built and cemented cesspool.

1832. May 22. The following, somewhat oddly worded notice, occurs in the records :

" * * of * * a patient leaves the Infirmary, at the present "time, on account of the very unhealthy state thereof, to be re-admitted "so soon as an improvement in the health of the Infirmary takes place."

Some improvement was shortly effected, for on

July 3rd, re-admissions were allowed.

1834. March 18. An order was given to open and inspect the cesspools and drains on the east and west sides of the building, and to clean out and ventilate the same, where necessary.

1837. May 2. A note is made—

"That the health of one of the nurses has suffered from the want of "ventilation in the building." and in

July, a plan for the better ventilation of the building was put forward by Mr. Browning, the Architect, and accepted.

Sept. 19. It was decided—

"To ventilate the water closets on the same plan as the wards and "other parts already done."

This is the first and only notice of any definite plan of ventilation of the building.

Scattered memoranda subsequently exist in the minutes, which show that defects, both in ventilation and sanitary arrangements, were from time to time reported, and dealt with. No great changes, however, seem to have been made until—

1860, Sept. when it is recorded that a plan for the reconstruction of the drains of the Infirmary, was sent in by Mr. Browning, considered and adopted. The plan provided for the entire abolition of the cesspools close to the building, for the formation of a new cesspool down to the rock on the margin of the Ryhall Road, north of the Infirmary, and for the carrying of special sanitary pipe drains from the various closets, and points of discharge, to this common centre.

1866. July. A lengthy report was sent in signed by the whole Medical Staff, of which the following is a short resumé :

" The attention of Committee is specially called to ventilation and drainage of Infirmary.

The Medical Staff have noted now for several years back :

1. Existence of outbreaks of Erysipelas in wards, after injuries and operations ;

2. Slow healing of wounds, and difficulty in keeping up general health, of cases admitted ;

3. Existence, not uncommonly, of cases of pyæmia (i.e. blood poisoning from absorption of putrid matters into circulation).

These three conditions form strongest ground for suspecting efficiency of both ventilation and drainage.

Necessary for satisfactory supply of air to any Hospital ward that there be—

(a) Due amount of cubic space to each bed ;

(b) Due provision for constant renewal of air contained in ward.

Under first head note, that each bed in an Hospital should have from 1000 to 1500 cubic feet of space; but in this Infirmary, with seven beds in each ward (see Table, No. 1, of cubic space), the allowance varies from 721—958 cubic feet. †

Under second head remark, that facilities for interchange of air are imperfect; ventilation arrangements by perforated iron plates in floors and ceilings of little value, windows small, and in middle and worst wards, not nearly up to the ceiling level.

Suggested therefore— .

That beds be reduced by *one* in each ward, so making total thirty-six. (adopted)

That one bed of the six, so retained, be kept empty, except in times of extreme emergency. (practically not adopted)

That Sheringham's ventilators be put into each ward close to the ceiling, and in outer wall of upper corridor. (inserted in corridors, and middle wards, not in lower wards)

---

† Two tables of the cubic capacity of the wards are appended (vide p. p. 38 39) the first quoted above, and based on the calculations and measurements of 1866, which further enquiry has proved to be incorrect ;

the second, made in 1878, by the clerk of the works for the new buildings, and strictly accurate in figures.

Both, however, point in the same direction, and the later table gives the more decided evidence of the absolute insufficiency of the cubic contents of the respective wards.

Drainage plan now in use consists of two huge pipe drains, from each end of building, conveying waste material to closed cesspool, on the Ryhall Road, but

No provision exists for preventing return into the house of injurious gases, always present in sewers ; that these gases do return, is proved by reference to conditions of water-closets, baths, and sinks ;

Suggested therefore—

That Syphon traps be placed in line of sewers, close outside walls, and special ventilating shafts be provided." (adopted)

Without doubt, the immediate effort of these changes was extremely good. The atmosphere of the house was sensibly improved, the patients were found to recover more rapidly, and fewer cases of blood-poisoning were noted.

But yet, when the wards were filled with occupants, and when there was for even a few days such bad weather that the windows could not be opened, it was at once evident that the air became close and unpleasant, and that the patients suffered in consequence. Especially was this the case in the mens' lower ward, and at night.

1875. Jan. An outbreak of erysipelas occurred, with many cases of severe sore throat, and the Medical Staff sent in a report which—

"Detailed the history of the cases, male and female, in the order of occurrence ; and pointed out that the probable causes of the outbreak were—

1. Introduction of the disease from without [several cases had been noted in neighbourhood] ;
2. Direct transmission by contaminated air, this much favoured by
   (a) Full tenancy of various beds ;
   (b) Close atmosphere of wards ;

and suggested—

Thorough cleaning and disinfection ;
Limitation of number of patients for a time ;
Special channels for removal of foul air from the wards."

These suggestions were adopted, and no further cases happened.

Exit shafts, guarded by louvres at the upper end, were accordingly placed in each ward, and at the inferior opening, flush with the ceiling of the ward, was placed in each instance an ordinary gas-jet. This could be lighted on occasion, and was found much to aid the upward current of out-going air.

1876. Sept. Two rectangular iron tubes, communicating below with the outer air and opening within the ward at the level of 4ft. 6in. above the floor, circular in section, and of 4in. diam. were placed in the mens' lower ward as an experiment; the purpose being to provide inlets for fresh air, which should be in constant action night and day, yet without creating draught.

1877. March. The effect of the above tubes was found to be very good. Four (including those already inserted) were consequently placed in the mens' lower ward, and three in each of the other wards.

The immediate result of the insertion of these inlets was an entire disappearance of the cases of so-called hospital sore throat. The resident Surgeon, had, with much care, taken note of the cases so suffering, and it had been found that hardly any patient admitted from Oct. 1876, to March, 1877, had completely escaped ; the younger and the more feeble the patient, the more severe the seizure ; in no instance had there been special ill consequences, but the general health of the patients had been much lowered and their convalescence very decidedly retarded.

About the same time the pipes from the baths and sinks, which had hitherto been carried into the main sewer without break, always, however, on the house side of the syphon traps, were absolutely disconnected and made to open upon trapped iron gratings, which in their turn led into the main sewer.

1877. Dec. The patients on the mens' side of the house, were, most of them, the subjects of a severe outbreak of diarrhœa, due, as further enquiry showed, to local subsidence, from fault in the subsoil, of that portion of the sewer lying just outside the house wall, with the sequence of retained excreta, and reflux of sewer odours. The necessary repairs were made as soon as the exact conditions were discovered, and immediately on their completion, the cases of this vexatious illness ceased.

The same enquiry showed that the special iron ventilating shafts, put up in 1866, were choked in the lower three feet of their length, with fine *débris* of granulated rust, the result of the slow action of damp air on the interior of the pipes. Proof positive, that for such purpose zinc, lead, or earthenware pipes, *and on no account iron*, should be employed.

Since the early part of the year just ended, the health conditions of the Infirmary have been good. If however the beds are fully occupied for more than a few days, and especially if there be any ready source of air-pollution from open wounds, the patients speedily suffer, and most of all those who are living in the middle wards.

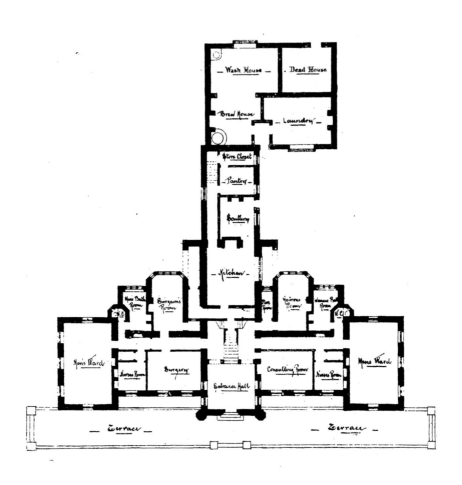

GROUND PLAN

Scale of Feet

THE writer of this notice has been given to understand, that the architect of the building was directed, in the first instance, so to construct the Infirmary that, if it failed in that purpose, it might readily be converted into a convenient dwelling house. This statement may, or may not, be true, but, at least, it will serve to illustrate how little the necessities of an Hospital were at that time realised by those who had the welfare of the sick members of the community much at heart, and who were anxiously using to that end, not only the professional knowledge of their architect, but also the ripe medical experience of their senior physician, the late Dr. Arnold.

Until however a comparatively recent date, it would seem that the designers and builders of hospitals were satisfied to take as their model, the plan of an ordinary residence ; giving additional bedroom accommodation to meet the wants of a largely increased number of inmates, and making the easy working of the administration, together with the personal comfort of the permanent residents, matters of paramount importance : with these purposes therefore grouping together, ' en bloc,' the wards for the patients, the necessary offices, and the rooms for the working staff ; but unhappily, in the so-doing, drifting away from the main object of the erection, viz. the care and well being of the sick.

Far too many of the older hospitals, and not a few even of the more recent ones, have been erected with this want of guiding principle, and exhibit faults in consequence which it is easy to note but extremely difficult to amend.

Thus, in such composite buildings, the atmosphere of the whole interior is common property, open to contamination alike by the exhalations from the bodies of invalid occupants, the preparation of food, the odours from ill-placed sanitary arrangements, and from any other, however undesirable, source of extraneous pollution.

For indeed, writing by the lights of the present day, it must be declared that the conditions of a dwelling house, and the needs of a building devoted to the care of the sick, though alike in essence, are very different in degree. That which is sufficient for the one, is by no means adequate to meet even the simplest requirements of the other.

Contrast, for one instant, the occupancy of the rooms of an average house, and of those of an hospital. Those of the house used day and night alternately, often and, even for some time unoccupied for any purpose, not as a rule crowded, with very frequent change of atmosphere, and with a variable number of tenants coming and going : the wards, on the other hand, continuously tenanted, not by healthy residents often absent, but by the sick and injured ; the living and sleeping rooms, at the same moment of a population which, rarely even comparatively scanty, is so only at the best time of year ; while directly that wet or wintry weather comes, every bed is occupied, from one good reason or another, and that at the very moment when due change, and sufficient purity of atmosphere, are to be obtained only with the greatest difficulty.

The inhabitants in the one case have no untoward personal conditions which can taint the surrounding atmosphere, but in the other, the emanations from the sick have very decided influence on the purity of the air, and in the course of time on even the very material of the walls and the floors of the various apartments so tenanted.

It will often be difficult to obtain sufficient air space, and sufficiently fresh air in most residences, how much more so to meet the demands of invalids ? To this end, the space occupied must be large, the supply of fresh air abundant, with every facility for thorough perflation, so that absolute change of air shall be readily accomplished, the warming effective, the sanitary arrangements perfect, and then only will be fairly met the primary needs of those who are actively ill, or slowly convalescing.

Advancing one step further, it may well be added that there is one word "isolation" which should be constantly, borne in mind in all buildings devoted to the sick; not that every case should have its separate apartment, but that such provisions should be made as to place in the hands of the medical staff the power, to be used at will and as need may arise, of effectively and thoroughly isolating any given case or series of cases.

As a matter of simple justice to the responsible authorities of years gone by, it should however be clearly pointed out that sanitary science, properly so-called, has but of late years made for itself an unquestioned position. The better knowledge of the requirements imperative in a well ordered Infirmary, dates little further back than the Crimean war, and year by year the data have become more precise and better understood. Although the details may be freely commented on, still the fullest recognition must be accorded to the spirit and earnestness with which the works of a preceding generation were undertaken and carried out.

To apply these remarks to the Stamford Infirmary, there can be little doubt that the earlier days of the Institution were the most favourable from a surgical point of view. The patients were few in number, and occupied only two terminal wards, to which they had access by well lighted and airy passages on the ground floor; the sanitary arrangements were, however, evidently far from being satisfactory.

As time passed by, the structural changes, which were decided on with the best purpose, brought more and more of building at the back of the Infirmary, and so rendered the access and change of air more uncertain and more difficult. The upper wards, corresponding in size and situation to the lower ones, were now slowly brought into full use, as the number of in-patients was increased.

Then came the introduction of a more complete system of sewerage, conveying the excreta some distance, but unhappily, without provision for the prevention of the return of sewer odours into the building.

Later still, when the provision of baths for the residents was deemed desirable, the proposal by the medical staff for a detached building on the north western face of the Infirmary, was not entertained, but a much more elaborate plan was adopted. This provided admirably for a new matron's room, and for an additional, consulting room, as well as for the necessary baths : but with the coincident and very serious drawback of blocking up the cross ventilation of all the water closets, and of limiting materially the access of air and light to the lower corridor on each side ; while the middle wards, very convenient in position, were yet made without provision for effective cross air-currents, and a far too narrow corridor completed the plan.

The additional space so found was unduly crowded with beds, and a glance, for the purpose of careful comparison, at the respective tables of cubic capacity and the number of in-patients actually allowed, will show how overcrowded the wards must have been (vide p.p. 38 39).

On this point the following quotation may be allowed to speak : *

" A careful measurement of the wards at this period showed, that in " many of them the space amounted to 780 cubic feet for each patient, and " that the average was not more than 980 cubic feet." A foot note to this paragraph thus continues—

" With regard to the question of cubic space, it may be well to remind " such of my readers as have but a slight acquaintance with sanitary science " that the object of providing a large cubic space, is not only to prevent " concentration of the emanations from the bodies of the patients, and so to " render them less noxious, but likewise to allow of the passage of a free

---

* 'A short account of the Old and the New Lincoln County Hospitals, by Thomas Sympson, F.R.C.S. Eng.

Lincoln, Williamson, 1878.

" current of air through the wards, without the production of perceptible
" draughts. The bodies of men and animals are constantly giving off certain
" products of the wear and tear of the tissues, which rapidly contaminate
" the surrounding atmosphere, and their products are increased in quantity
" and offensiveness, when the bodies from which they are derived are
" suffering from disease. Hence, the necessity for a large cubic space in
" hospital wards becomes apparent, a space of not less than 1,400 or 1,500,
" cubic feet. This may be illustrated by stating, that a room 15 feet long,
" 10 feet wide, and 10 feet high, contains 1,500 cubic feet."

Shortly afterwards, however, one bed was removed from each middle ward; and two years subsequently, after some sad lessons of the unhealthiness of the building, the total number of beds was again lessened, one bed again being deducted from each ward.

At the same time also, changes were made in the sanitary arrangements of the closets with great resulting good, and special ventilators were introduced.

Some years subsequently, it was decided to attempt to make each ward more independent of the general atmosphere of the house ; and on this view an exit channel was fixed in each ward communicating directly with the external air : while a little later still inlets for air were introduced with marked benefit.

THE new wards are situated east of the older building, a space of from forty to fifty yards intervening between them. Three blocks of two stories each afford on each floor accommodation for *five* patients and a nurse ; these blocks are practically uniform in arrangement, the central block differing, however, somewhat in external appearance and in the internal plan from the other two ; a distance of from seven to ten yards exists between the several blocks.

Behind these structures is an open space, fifty yards deep, left purposely for the erection at some future time, if it be found desirable, of a kitchen, or other offices. At the further end of this space is placed a low one-storied building, containing the appliances for a laundry and disinfecting chamber, while in the rear of this again is the dead-house, also quite detached.

To go more into details : especial care was taken to cover all the enclosed area with a layer of Portland cement concrete, six inches thick, so as to prevent the ascent of damp from the subjacent porous oolitic strata. A damp-proof course was also provided at the base of the walls.

The buildings are of the local stone of the district, oolitic, of varying density. The quoins, jambs, and window-beads are of Casterton stone, the window-sills, and plinths of Clipsham limestone.

Each block, to speak of one for all, has two stories above the ground-level, and in the basement more or less of cellar room, for storage of coal, &c. Each story is thus arranged :—There is an entrance lobby, having on one side the stone staircase, and on the other side a nurse's room, while between the two is placed the door of the ward, which, with its appendages, occupies the remaining space.

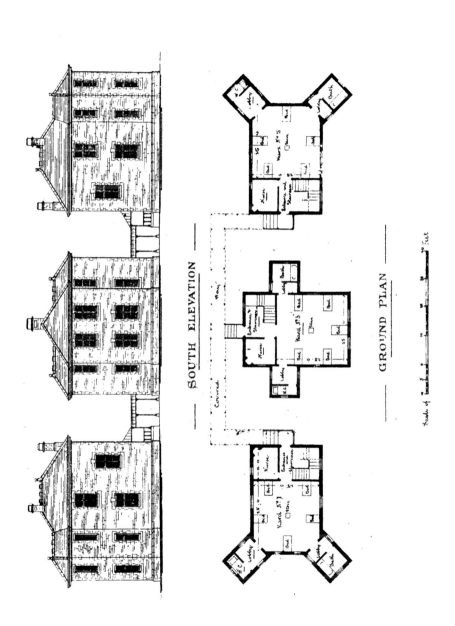

— SOUTH ELEVATION —

— GROUND PLAN —

Scale of ┠┄┄┄┄┄┄┄┄┄┄┄┄┄┄┄┄┄┄┄┄┄ Feet

The ward is twenty-five feet square, with a height of fifteen feet, and is arranged to receive *five* patients : the air-space for each bed therefore being over 1,800 cubic feet. The walls are lined with glazed bricks throughout, built in as the work proceeded, and jointed in Parian cement with the purpose of making the walls impermeable and absolutely non-retentive of organic matters.

The windows are placed on the three outer sides of the ward ; two, smaller in size, face the door of entrance, while the larger windows on the right and left hand respectively are directly opposite to each other. In their lower two-thirds the windows are of the ordinary sash-pattern, while the upper third is occupied by a framed casement, which is hinged at the bottom and falls inward at pleasure. This arrangement has been adopted in all the windows.

Each ward has a bath room and water-closet, opening, with the intervention of a cross-ventilated lobby, from the corners most distant from the entrance door. This description applies to the two end blocks only ; in the central structure the bath-room and water-closet are on the right and left of the entrance door in the corners of the return walls. These additions are lined with Parian cement ; the stair case, nurse's room, &c., with ordinary plaster.

Four rectangular metal ventilating shafts for the supply of fresh air are fitted in each ward, opening below the floor level to the external air, and ending within the ward about five feet above the floor.

A central stove on Galton's pattern is placed in the ward ; to this fresh air is brought by special wide channels from the out_side, and this air, warmed in its passage, is delivered into the room through perforated openings above the stove, three feet from the floor. The smoke-flue is continued straight upwards to the open air, running within a square framing of metal-work covered with tiles : not quite one half of the sectional area of this framing is, however, occupied by the smoke-flues ; the remaining portion is so contrived as to form a ventilating shaft for the two wards, extracting by special gratings the foul and heated air close under the ceiling, and then delivering it through openings of proportionate size placed on the sides of the chimney some distance above the roof.

The entrances and the nurses' rooms are paved with hard, well-burned red and black Staffordshire tiles; the ward floor is of hard pitch pine, long dried before use, and closely joined by grooved and tongued joints; it is intended, by coating of paraffin or varnish, to make these floors impermeable to moisture. Under all these wooden floors there is provision for the free circulation of air between the concrete below and the joints above.

The whole of the internal woodwork has been so arranged that there are no mouldings or projections round the doors or windows; no facilities, in short, for the collection of dust. The woodwork again internally is all varnished, not painted.

The glazed linings of the ward have been thus planned:—Next the floor are placed two courses of black bricks; then a dado, about four feet high, of cream-coloured bricks, finished above by a single band of chocolate colour; from this darker line to the ceiling the wall is covered with bricks of greyish white. To break the uniformity and coldness of this colour, three tile pictures (three feet by two feet) have been placed, one on the inner face of each external wall. These pictures illustrate in each instance some agricultural or outdoor occupation, and are let in flush with the inner surface of the wall itself.

In the lobby of the bath-room is fitted a plain slate lavatory. The baths in most of the wards will be on wheels, so as to allow of easy movement to the bedside of any inmate.

The closets are throughout on Jennings' trapless pattern; they open directly without syphon or bend into an earthenware soil-pipe, constructed of jointed lengths of glazed sanitary pipes, specially made for the purpose. The upper end of the soil-pipe open to the external air, is guarded by a Field's cowl, and the channel, fixed to the outside of the wall, discharges below into a main sewer, with the intervention, close outside the wall, of a Potts' Edinburgh trap.

All the waste-pipes from closets, cisterns, or baths, from sinks in the nurses' rooms, or lavatories, are so constructed as to ensure perfect disconnection ; in each instance they are carried through the outer walls, run down the outside, and open upon hollowed stones a foot or more distant from a trapped iron grating lying upon the ground level : sewer gas, if it should regurgitate through the traps, cannot therefore ascend through these pipes into the building.

The branches of sewer from each closet, bath-room, and surface trap are collected into one large channel, which leads down to a closed but yet well-ventilated cesspool. This is fitted with convenient arrangement on the ground-level for such frequent emptying as may be desired. In the line of the main sewer, 140 yards in length, there are two or more apertures for the escape of sewer gas.

The disinfecting apparatus which has been selected, is on the pattern suggested by Dr. Ransom of Nottingham.

The whole arrangements have been carefully worked out by Mr. Browning, the architect, of Stamford. The exterior is extremely plain, with no elaborate ornamentation, and the internal arrangements at least allow the hope that perfect isolation, with every convenience for the sick inmates, will have been attained.

MEDICAL OFFICERS.

Consulting Physicians—

Thomas Graham Arnold, M.D., Edin.	Elected Jan. 21, 1843.	Died Feb. 23, 1855.
William Landen Hopkinson, M.D., Edin.	,, Jan. 9, 1866.	,, June 24, 1875.

Physicians—

Thomas Graham Arnold, M.D., Edin.	Elected July 21, 1827.	Resigned Sept. 20, 1842.
William Landen Hopkinson, M.D., Edin.	,, July 21, 1827.	,, Jan. 9, 1866.
Alexander Rozel Brown, M.D., Cantab.	,, Sept. 20, 1842.	,, May 15, 1849.
Spencer Pratt, M.D., Edin., M.R.C.P.	,, Jan. 13, 1852.	,, March 31, 1866.
Offley Bohun Shore, M.D., Edin.	,, Jan. 2, 1866.	left Stamford March 1866.

Assistant Physician—

Spencer Pratt, M.D., Edin., M.R.C.P.	Elected June 19, 1849.	Elected Physician Jan. 13, 1852.

Acting Physician—

George Frederick Elliott, M.D., Dublin.	From April 1866.	Until Oct. 1867. Then left Stamford.

MEDICAL OFFICERS *(continued)*.

CONSULTING SURGEONS—

Benjamin Cooper.	Elected July 21, 1827.	Died April 18, 1842.
William Burdett, M.R.C.S.	,, Jan. 11, 1853.	,, April 11, 1867.

SURGEONS—

John Geo. De Merveilleux, M.R.C.S.	Elected Oct. 11, 1827.	Died Oct. 1843.
Mark Wilson Jackson, F.R.C.S.	,, Oct. 11, 1827.	,, July 4, 1862.
William Burdett, M.R.C.S.	,, Oct. 11, 1827.	Resigned Sept. 21, 1852.
William Whitby, M.R.C.S.	,, Oct. 11, 1827.	Died May 25, 1837.
Edward Hatfield, M.R.C.S.	,, Oct. 11, 1827.	,, Oct. 5, 1852.
Edward Barber, M.R.C.S.	,, Jan. 11, 1853.	,, Feb. 13, 1860.
Charles Simpson, M.R.C.S.	,, Jan. 11, 1853.	,, March 31, 1857.
Robert Nicholas Newcomb, M.R.C.S.	,, Jan. 11, 1853.	Resigned in 1853.
Walter Dowley Eddowes, M.R.C.S.	,, March 13, 1860.	
Fortescue John Morgan, M.R.C.S.	,, March 13, 1860.	Resigned July 29, 1873.
John Mitchell Heward, M.R.C.S.	,, March 13, 1860.	
William Edward Robbs, M.B., Lond., M.R.C.S.	,, July 29, 1862.	Resigned April 21, 1873.
William Newman, M.D., Lond., F.R.C.S.	,, Jan. 9, 1866.	
Fortescue John Morgan, M.R.C.S.	Re-elected Jan. 10, 1876.	
William Edward Robbs, M.B., Lond., M.R.C.S.	,, Jan. 10, 1876.	Declined the appointment.

MEDICAL OFFICERS *(continued).*

HOUSE SURGEONS—

Edward Brown,	Elected Oct. 11, 1827.	Died Jan. 3, 1838.
William Hughes, M.R.C.S. L.S.A.	,, Feb. 20, 1838.	Resigned Jan. 1846.
Edward Walker Woodcock, M.R.C.S. L.S.A.	,, Jan. 13, 1846.	,, Sept. 16, 1851.
Henry William Bromley, M.R.C.S. L.S.A.	,, Jan. 13, 1852.	,, Jan. 8, 1856.
Wm. Robert Faun Marchant, M.D.St.And.M.R.C.S.	,, Jan. 18, 1856.	,, Jan. 13, 1857.
John Cooke, M.R.C.S. L.S.A.	,, Jan. 13, 1857.	,, Nov. 22, 1859.
Charles Henry Drake, M.R.C.S. L.S.A.	,, Jan. 10, 1860.	,, Sept. 2, 1862.
Clement Winstanley, M.R.C.S. L.S.A.	,, Oct. 14, 1862.	,, March 21, 1865.
George Grewcock, M.R.C.S. L.S.A.	,, April 18, 1865.	,, Jan. 7, 1867.
James Rew, M.R.C.S. L.S.A.	,, Feb. 5, 1867.	,, March 12, 1870.
Joseph Goodall, M.R.C.S. L.R.C.P.	,, April 12, 1870.	,, Dec. 1870.
Alfred Thomas Gibbings, M.B., Lond., M.R.C.S.	,, Jan. 10, 1871.	,, June 14, 1873.
Thomas Decimus Paradise, M.R.C.S. L.S.A.	,, July 29, 1873.	,, March 7, 1876.
Thomas Porter Greenwood, M.R.C.S.	,, March 7, 1876.	,, Dec. 10, 1878.
William More Hope, M.R.C.S. L.S.A.	,, Jan. 7, 1879.	

OFFICERS *(continued).*

CHAPLAINS—

Rev. Denis Edward Jones, B.A.	Elected Oct. 2, 1849.	Resigned April 14, 1877.
Rev. William Christopher Houghton, B.A.	,, May 15, 1877.	

MATRONS—

Mrs. Susanna Clarke	Elected Oct. 11, 1827.	Resigned July 23, 1831.
Miss Eliza Simpson	,, Sept. 20, 1831.	,, Sept. 13, 1859.
Miss Eliza Lovell	,, Sept. 13, 1859.	Died Aug. 5, 1869.
Miss Sarah Hissett	,, Oct. 26, 1869.	

PORTERS—

John Worsdale	Elected Oct. 11, 1827.	Dismissed Oct. 13, 1829.
Thomas Blades	,, Oct. 13, 1829.	Resigned Dec. 20, 1836.
John Hissett	,, Jan. 10, 1837.	

TABULAR STATEMENT OF BEDS OCCUPIED IN DIFFERENT WARDS.

		Men.			Women.		
		Lower.	Upper.	Middle.	Lower.	Upper.	Middle
From 1828—1836.	12 Beds.	6	-	-	6	-	-
,, 1837—1842.	18 ,,	6	3	-	6	3	-
,, 1843—1852.	21 ,,	6	6	-	6	3	-
,, 1854—1861.	24 ,,	6	6	-	6	6	-
,, 1862—1864.	44 ,,	7	7	8	7	7	8
,, 1865—1866.	42 ,,	7	7	7	7	7	7
,, 1867 to present time	36 ,,	6	6	6	6	6	6

CUBIC CAPACITY OF WARDS.

TABLE NO. I.
1866.

	Eight Beds. Space to each Bed.	Seven Beds. Space to each Bed.	Six Beds. Space to each Bed.	Five Beds. Space to each Bed.
Lower Ward contains 5753 cubic feet.		958	948	1150
Middle ,, 5048 ,,	631	721	841	1009
Upper ,, 5436 ,,		776	907	1087

TABLE NO. 2.
1878.

	Eight Beds. Space to each Bed.	Seven Beds. Space to each Bed.	Six Beds. Space to each Bed.	Five Beds. Space to each Bed.
Lower Ward contains 5326 cubic feet.	604.6	760.8	887.6	1065.2
Middle ,, 4839 ,,		691.2	806.5	967.8
Upper ,, 5919 ,,		845.5	989.8	1183.8

PRINTED BY JENKINSON & SONS, 58, HIGH STREET, STAMFORD.

HISTORY OF THE STAMFORD AND RUTLAND HOSPITAL

**Commissioned to mark the 150th anniversary
by the Friends of Stamford Hospital, 1978**

1828-1978

.

A SHORT HISTORY

OF

THE STAMFORD
AND RUTLAND HOSPITAL

The Friends of the Stamford Hospitals

(Affiliated to the National Association of Leagues of Hospital Friends)

Patrons:
The Most Hon. The Marquess of Exeter, K.C.M.G.
The Right Hon. The Earl of Ancaster, K.C.V.O.

This book has been published to celebrate the 150th Anniversary of our Hospital. It has been compiled by Dr Alan Rogers and John Quinlan of the Stamford Survey Group.

The original suggestion came from Dr Leslie Holt, who has assisted them. Valuable help with the early history of the hospital has been given by David Curnyn.

To all concerned we offer our grateful thanks.

THE STAMFORD AND RUTLAND HOSPITAL

We live in an age where the State plays the role of a benevolent parent caring for our sick, with free hospitalisation, cheap medicine, expert nursing and surgical skills available to all its members. The grisly spectre of the poor, begging for alms in order to keep body and soul together, with nothing but rags and tattered clothing to protect them from the inclement weather, has almost disappeared from our streets, and we are no longer obliged to make provision for the rainy day when it might be necessary for us to pay to receive even elementary medical attention. Our children are born under ideal conditions in our modern well equipped hospitals, to mothers who have received every care and expert treatment in our pre-natal clinics. The older members of our community, can enter the twilight of their lives, secure in the knowledge that there will always be a social service to administer to their needs when they are no longer able to cope with the everyday chores of old age. It has not always been so; these changes did not take place overnight, but came about gradually, the result of long years of unstinted devotion, foresight and effort in the past on the part of certain dedicated members of our community towards their fellow men.

1

A past not so long past, surprisingly, only one hundred and fifty years ago. What a shining reward would be theirs if those visionaries could but see the fruits of their tireless perseverance. Such a visionary was Henry Fryer, a Stamfordian who died in 1823, leaving amongst others a bequest for the building of an infirmary in Stamford.

Like so many other provincial towns of its size in the Middle Ages, Stamford boasted a number of small hospitals, the largest of these, Brownes Hospital was founded in 1475 by Letters Patent of Richard III. They were established by the more prosperous members of the community during their life times, and endowed by others after their death, as permanent reminders of their importance in the community, and possibly as a sop to their consciences to do something useful for their fellow men, after they had passed on.

These hospitals were established primarily for the old and infirm, and for the use of travellers and pilgrims who might be passing through the town, in order that they would have somewhere to rest their weary limbs and spend the night. It is very probable that these and the various monastic establishments in the town would have been involved to some extent in the welfare of the townspeople by providing succour to the needy and comfort to the sick.

With the dissolution of the monasteries in 1539, Stamford was left without any form of communal medicine and would have been at the mercy of the various apothecaries and surgeons who practised their doubtful forms of healing in many parts of the town. The occasional arrival of fairs visiting Stamford brought in their wake the usual quota of faith healers, and numerous dentists and quack doctors. Dentists as we know them today were of course unknown and the task of drawing teeth was often left to the skill of the local blacksmith.

On his death, Henry Fryer's estate amounted to nearly £21,000, and as he had never married, this money was distributed by his will between his many close friends, and twenty worthy Institutions, including the Clergy of Lincoln and Peterborough, the Bluecoat and Stamford

Schools, Churches, Sunday Schools, the Christian Knowledge Society and a large sum was given for the founding of Fryer's Hospital on the Kettering Road. Like his father he had been a surgeon and had practised his skill in the town, living in a small house rented from Lord Exeter at 8/5d a week. His needs were simple and were catered for by his housekeeper Anne Smith and his manservant George Rawlinson, both of whom were remembered in his Will.

The residue of Fryer's estate amounted to £7,477 after taking account of his specific bequests and was to be used to build a General Infirmary in Stamford, provided it was built within five years of his death. If it was not built within the specific time, the money was to go to several alternative charities, including the Lincoln County Hospital, Northampton General Hospital, Leicester Infirmary, Middlesex Hospital and St. George's Hospital in London.

Two years after Fryer's death, a public meeting was held at the town hall on 2nd July 1825 to consider the bequest and how it should be implemented. The outcome of the meeting was a decision to build a hospital sufficiently large enough to accommodate twenty in-patients. At the same meeting a committee consisting of eighteen local worthies was formed to make the necessary arrangements. A few weeks later this number was increased to thirty-two with the Marquess of Exeter as Chairman. The involvement of the Exeter family in the founding of the infirmary and its subsequent development was substantial and it seems possible, that were it not for the interest the family took the infirmary's development might not have been so rapid. Successive Marquesses were Chairmen of the hospital committee until 1948.

This new committee had many tasks to face, one of the most important of which was to raise additional funds by means of subscriptions and donations. Although the money left by Fryer was sufficient to build an infirmary, money was still needed to meet its running costs, and it is important to note that in its early days the infirmary was a charitable institution as were the town's alms houses and schools. All of these relied on the beneficence of the more well-to-do Stamfordians, many of whom would never derive any direct benefit from their charitable impulses. That the town managed to support so many charities at all speaks volumes for the outward piety of upper class Victorians.

By July 1825 the committee was sufficiently organised to approach five London architects with a request that they draw up plans for:
> 'A building to contain not less than 20 patients and be capable of conveniently accommodating 32 if necessary.'

The building was to be constructed with local stone quarried at Wittering or Barnack, all quoins, heads, sills and jambs to be of Ketton stone. The foundations were to be of Stamford stone laid in Stamford lime. It was rumoured at the time that the architects were also given instructions to design the building in such a way that if the charity failed it could easily be turned into a private house.

At this stage in the development of the new infirmary the committee began to experience problems. There was dissatisfaction in certain quarters and arguments raged over the size of the infirmary, the number of beds and even whether it should accommodate both sexes. In addition to this there were problems with the architects. Of the five architects approached to provide designs for the building, four had responded in the usual professional manner. The fifth, Mr. George Basevi, had been a friend of Henry Fryer and refused to compete for the project, claiming that Fryer had promised him complete charge of all buildings financed by him under the terms of his Will. This view was upheld by the executors of the Will who informed the committee that it would be wrong not to accept this claim. The committee however dismissed his claim, and Basevi took no further part in the project but went on to design Fryer's Hospital in 1832, and designs by him were also used for the re-building of Truesdale's Hospital in the same year.

The four remaining architects submitted plans of varying design and cost.

J. P. Gandy	A Gothic design costing £4,000
H. E. Kendal	A Norman design costing £4,800
L. Valliamy	A Gothic design costing £4,500
J. Ireland	A Grecian design costing £4,580

Of these, the designs submitted by Gandy and Ireland were short listed, and after much debate by the Committee Gandy's design was finally adopted by twenty votes to nine.

In September 1825 it had been decided by the Committee that the most suitable site for the infirmary was the triangle of land between the Ryhall and Uffington roads. About two and half acres of this land was subsequently purchased from the Marquess of Exeter at a price estimated to be well below its market value.

The occupation of this site has traditionally been attributed to the house of the Carmelites or White Friars of Stamford, but from the available evidence it seems almost certain that it was in fact occupied by the Grey Friars (Franciscans) until the dissolution of the monasteries. All that remains today is the 14th Century Gateway which was the original entrance to the Friary. It must have presented a much more ornate appearance when three niches with their pinnacled canopies were occupied by the figures of its benefactors. There are three shields, of Norman shape, very weather-beaten, two of which bear the figures of the lions or leopards of England and the Fleur de Lys of France, but the third is wholly defaced.

According to Francis Peck, the most important historian of Stamford who was writing in the 18th Century, the Church of the monastery was especially beautiful, having a spire similar to that of All Saints Church in Stamford.

In addition to the usual beggars and homeless seeking alms and shelter, many interesting and important personages entered these gates. It is thought that Cardinal Wolsey sheltered in the monastery for one night on his journey to York whence he had been banished by Henry VIII.

After the dissolution, the property passed through the hands of Charles Brandon, Duke of Suffolk, when the main buildings were demolished, and then to Thomas Cleghorn, who sold it to Sir William Cecil of Burghley in 1561. It is interesting to note that on 5th August 1565 William Cecil recorded in his diary that Queen Elizabeth "was entertained at my house, the Grey Friary, because my daughter Ann was suddenly seized with the smallpox at Burghley".

The actual construction of the new Infirmary was undertaken by a Mr. Crowe of Peterborough, and by the middle of 1826 his firm had begun work on the foundations. During the excavations of the cellars, a reminder of the site's former occupants was found in the form of thirty human skulls. These were found at between three and four feet below the surface and some two feet apart with the crowns pointing to the west. The ground on which the foundations were dug was the site on which the former monastic church had stood.

Funds continued to come in for the building of the hospital, as work progressed; these were being raised mainly by the efforts of townspeople in organising various charities and balls, fetes and markets in aid of the institution. The most ambitious venture was that put forward by Mr. Richard Sharpe of St. George's Square, who suggested to the committee that a ball and concert patronised by the Marquess of Exeter and the Earl of Winchelsea and Nottingham, from neighbouring Burley on the Hill, would be sure to draw crowds and swell the funds. It was decided to hold such a function at the Assembly Rooms in Stamford, and preparations went ahead. No expense appeared to have been spared in obtaining the best available talent for the occasion. A thirty-six piece Philharmonic Orchestra was hired, supported by famous Italian Opera stars such as Tignosina Fortunata, Malanimi and Angasapio, which attracted a large fashionable crowd from far and near to hear their rendering of songs and arias from Rossini, Bishop and Crouch, and the music of Mozart, Weber and Beethoven. Unfortunately the cost of engaging all this talent ate into the profits, with the net result that only £17 was raised at the end of the day. The event was fully reported in the Stamford Mercury, but Stamfordians were not impressed by this lavish expenditure which netted so small a return.

The whole process of raising money was to be a continuous one, and formed a permanent part of the committee's activities. In the ensuing years many similar bazaars and functions were held for this purpose. The main-stay of the hospital was however, private individuals who undertook to make annual subscriptions to the charity. In the first year of the Infirmary's existence, there were some 262 subscribers in the Stamford area.

The subscribers to the Infirmary met on 26th April 1828 for the first time in a General Meeting, with the Marquess of Exeter taking the chair, to adopt rules for the future working of the Infirmary. This meeting was adjourned until July of that year, and on that occasion the first consulting medical staff were appointed, two physicians and a consulting surgeon.

The two physicians appointed were Dr. Graham Arnold and Dr. William Hopkinson, both from the Edinburgh Medical School and the Surgeon Mr. Benjamin Cooper. The Matron was a middle-aged lady by the name of Suzannah Clarke, her only qualifications being that she had been a housekeeper to many well-known families around the Stamford area. She does not appear to have had any nursing qualifications. The first porter was a man by the name of John Worsdale, who despite indifferent references from the Marquess of Exeter, his former employer, was elected to the post by 15 votes to 4. The clergymen living in and around Stamford offered their names as being willing to help in giving spiritual guidance and in reading prayers to the in-patients, and a rota for such duties was drawn up. It was recorded in the minutes of this meeting that the sum expended on the erection of the building had been £5,793 12s. 1d. Further amounts, however, were needed for providing certain internal fittings and for the furnishing of the wards.

In March 1828 a bazaar was held in Stamford in aid of the funds of the Infirmary, and a substantial amount of £1,768 was raised. The building was opened for the reception of the first patients on 5th August 1828, and 12 in-patients appear to have been admitted. The records show that the Hospital building could accommodate up to 20 patients — 10 men and 10 women — and also show in some detail the actual ground and first floor plans which include the surgery, consulting room, Matron's room, Surgeon's room, and also a wash house, a mortuary, a laundry and strangely enough a brew-house. The provision of a brew-house is most interesting and appears to be one of the more important rooms in the Hospital, especially when it is realised that expenditure on drugs for the year 1829 was somewhere in the region of £45, whereas expenditure on hops, beer, spirits and wines was in excess of £40; the reason for its existence was to cater for the daily allowance of one and a half pints of beer to each patient.

Like all other Institutions, certain rules and orders had to be laid down governing the running of the Stamford and Rutland Infirmary, and some of the more interesting ones follow. Administration was to be through a committee consisting of the President, Vice-President and Governors; the first President was the Most Noble, the Marquess of Exeter, K.G., Lord Lieutenant of the Country of Rutland. The Vice-Presidents were usually made up of the High Sheriff of the County and representatives of Parliament for the County, and also the Borough of Stamford Councillors. The Governors were made up of those persons who were willing to donate twenty guineas at any one time to the Hospital. Such a donation made that person a Governor for life. There was a general meeting of all Governors twice a year, and also a weekly Board Meeting consisting of three Governors held every Tuesday at 11 a.m. to regulate all matters relating to the administration and discharge of patients. One of these Governors, who resided in or near Stamford, was appointed at every weekly Board to visit the Infirmary for the week ensuing, as often as may be convenient to him, in order to enquire into the conduct of the patients and servants, and to enforce the observance of morality and attention to the rules and orders of the Infirmary. Rules governing employees were quite often harsh. For instance, no one was allowed to be an employee of the Hospital if they had children and the care of a family, and when first elected or hired they were not allowed to be above the age of 50; when proposed as candidates they had to produce certificates of age. Any nurse or person found guilty of taking any sort of fee or gratuity from a patient or tradesman was instantly dismissed. Although treatment was free, the method of gaining admission as a patient to the Hospital was not easy. One either had to know a subscriber or be a subscriber oneself. The rules stated that donors of 10 guineas would be entitled to recommend one out-patient annually, whereas donors of 20 guineas or subscribers of one guinea yearly would be entitled to recommend two out-patients annually. The more money that one donated, the more out-patients and in-patients one was entitled to recommend.

Patients were usually admitted and discharged every Tuesday at the weekly Board Meeting of Governors between the hours of 11 a.m. and 1 p.m. No horse or cart bringing a patient to the Infirmary was allowed to leave until it was known whether the patient could be admitted or not. No children under the age of 8, except in cases where an operation was to be performed, and no pregnant women were to be admitted as in-patients, neither were any persons disordered in their senses, subject to fits, or those having small-pox, itch or venereal disease, consumption or an incurable state of dropsy.

In 1832 there appeared to have been an epidemic of cholera in Stamford, and no one suffering from this complaint was allowed anywhere near the Hospital. No patient would be admitted to the Infirmary unless he presented himself in decent clothing — and also with a proper change of linen.

Another rule was that any in-patient or out-patient who did not derive any benefit from treatment within two months should be discharged;

those patients who were discharged cured were expected to join the Chairman of the weekly Board of Governors in prayer to give thanks to Almighty God for their deliverance.

The staff of the Hospital was a fairly small one and consisted of a consultant physician and two surgeons. Later on because of economies one surgeon was dispensed with.

The physician and surgeon usually made their rounds every Tuesday morning at 10 a.m. and this was the only time they visited the wards. In between times they attended to their practices in Stamford and also performed operations at the hospital. The next member of the Hospital staff, Edward Brown, was fulltime, and he was known as the House Apothecary-cum-Secretary, as these two offices were combined. The salary of the House Apothecary was £60 per annum with board and lodging, and he was allowed £20 yearly for his services as the Secretary. His duty as House Apothecary was to draw up a weekly account of the in-patients and affix a ticket on each patient's bed showing his name and the name of the physician or the surgeon attending. He made a bed count at the end of each week and visited the wards twice a day at 9.30 in the morning and 6 in the evening, and was prepared each time to report the state of the patients to the respective physician or surgeon. His duties as Secretary were to attend every meeting and minute and register all proceedings, and always be ready to produce the books and the accounts of the Infirmary, neatly written. He had to keep a register and enter all the names of the in-patients and the out-patients, the Parish to which they belonged, their age, date of admission and discharge, and the state of their health. His duties involved him in the purchase of medical instruments and drugs. In addition he also acted as storeman, receptionist, and public relations officer. He had to notify the clergyman every fortnight as to whose turn it was to read the prayers, and send regular accounts to the Stamford newspapers with the weekly bed state. An inventory of all household goods, including furniture belonging to the Infirmary, had to be maintained, with a copy to the Matron. He had to keep an alphabetical list of benefactors and subscribers showing the amount of their subscriptions, and when they had been paid; he also acted as Treasurer and had to keep a fair cash book in which all the sums received or paid by him were entered and the books balanced at every General Meeting.

He is commemorated by a Memorial Stone inset into the west wall of All Saints Church Stamford, which reads:

Sacred to the Memory of
EDWARD BROWN
The first House Surgeon and Apothecary to the
Stamford and Rutland Infirmary the laborious duties of which
appointment he discharged for a period of nine years with
indefatigable zeal and assiduity. His talents and professional
attainments were of a superior order and he devoted them
unsparingly to the welfare of those committed to his charge.

He died January 3 A.D. 1838 aged 37 years. In the blessed
hope of everlasting life through the merits of his Saviour
Jesus Christ.

The Matron of the Hospital received £25 p.a. in addition to board and lodging, when the hospital first opened. This sum was later increased to £30 p.a. during the early 1840's. Her main jobs, in order of priority, were that she had to take care of all the household goods and furniture, and be prepared to give an account whenever required to the Weekly Board of Governors; she also had to keep a daily account of all the provisions and other necessaries brought into the Infirmary, ready to lay before the Weekly Board, and was obliged to attend the weighing and measuring of the goods. She was also responsible, of course, for the well being of the patients and the nursing staff. She had to maintain diet books and make sure that each patient received the appropriate diet. Her responsibilities also extended to keeping all the keys of the doors of the Hospital and seeing that each door was locked and the keys brought to her by the porter at 9 o'clock in the summer and 7 o'clock in the winter.

The nurses employed, usually by the Matron, were really not nurses at all because their main duties were to clean the wards by 7 o'clock in the morning from 1st March to 1st October and by 8 o'clock in the morning during the winter — October to March. The main rule in the order book, 'No. 1', was that the 'nurses and servants shall obey the Matron as the mistress and behave with kindness to the patients and give attention to strangers'.

The porter also had a variety of jobs, he visited the wards usually twice a day, strictly to regulate the conduct and duty of the patients and servants. As well as obeying the orders of the physicians and surgeons, the apothecary and the matron, he had to do the labouring work of the house, and after he had finished that, if there was any time, he had to keep the yard clean and attend to the garden. In those days, of course, there was no such thing as an annual holiday. The staff of the Hospital were allowed one day off per week and they were never allowed to take more than one day in succession — this rule included the surgeon and apothecary.

This account is but a bare outline of the beginnings of Stamford Infirmary, and the surviving records go into much more interesting detail. The medical and surgical cases which were received by the Infirmary were fairly mixed and probably compare with the type of patient one would see in a General Hospital today. For the year ending 1830, there were 5 cases of enteric fever, one of dysentery, one case of scarlet fever, one case of cancer of the stomach, 10 cases of anaemia, and one case of diabetes. It is difficult to say whether or not these were extreme cases and had to be admitted to hospital because they were terminal. There were also 11 cases of diseases of the nervous system, 4 cases of heart disease, 8 cases of lung disease, 2 cases of stomach ulcers, 1 case of liver disease, 1 case of parasitic disease and 2 cases of unknown causes, together with 12 cases of general debility.

1830 must have been a very violent year because there were 35 admissions for wounds to the person. These may of course have been wounds obtained during work, but the records show that there were

4 suicidal injuries of the neck, 2 suicidal injuries of the chest, 1 fractured spine, 1 fractured pelvis and 5 injuries of "upper extremity", wounds and contusions. 52 minor operations were performed, the most difficult one appearing to be "removal of an upper limb", which occurred once. The usual type of operation was for removal of a tumour, cancer of the lip, tongue or face, nasal polyp, cataract operations and amputations of the hand; as an anaesthetic, nitrous oxide gas was given twice during this year, chloroform was given 5 times and ether 40 times.

The main donations to the Hospital between 1829 and 1830 were £1,700 from the proceeds of a bazaar at Stamford, £1,400 from the Rutland Yeomanry Fund, £300 from the Ness Yeomanry Troop, and many other donations from churches, theatrical performances at Stamford, and one of £7 from the Market Deeping Association for the Prosecution of Felons.

Additions to the infirmary buildings have continued piecemeal almost to the present day. In February 1842 the Governors decided to add to the buildings and enlarge the kitchen at an estimated cost of £300. Mr. Rowles of Stilton died in 1847 leaving a sum of £11,285 to the Infirmary, and seven years later, in 1849, a Mrs. Hodson of Stamford died and bequeathed £200 towards the cost of erecting a porter's lodge. The lodge, which was to be built on to the original mediaeval gateway, was designed by Mr. Clutton and built by Thompson and Ruddle of Peterborough; it was erected in the same year at a cost of £367. The wash house and adjoining buildings were further enlarged in 1852. In 1860 the Medical Officers of the Infirmary sent a report to the Governors urging that hot and cold baths be provided for the patients. The next year plans were submitted by Mr. Browning for the erection of bathrooms on either side of the main building, the provision of a new surgery and matron's room and for increasing the size of the middle wards. The cost of this work was estimated at £730.

Towards the middle of 1875 notice was given to the Committee that a considerable amount of money had been bequeathed to the Infirmary by the late Mr. Arthur Clay, a surgeon and a member of a very old Stamford family. He had died recently in Japan. There was some confusion at the time because the actual will of Mr. Clay stated that he was a trader in a place called Kobihiobo in Japan and that he had made all his money out of tea; there is no mention of him being medically qualified at all. The Hospital received £3,500 from Mr. Clay's Will, but it was not easy to accept because the Chaplain of the Day objected at one of the Committee meetings that there was a rumour that Clay, although making his money out of tea, had used an army of slave labour and, of course, the Church was not at all happy about this. In the end Lord Exeter decided to ignore the Chaplain and accepted the money on behalf of the Infirmary.

The year 1876 was an important one in the development of the Infirmary. In April of that year it was decided that there should be an extension to accommodate persons suffering from infectious diseases other than small-pox. This major decision had been taken as a result of the 1875 Public Health Act. Another far reaching decision was to allow the Managing Committee to admit patients "above the class of those at present admitted", on condition that they paid for maintenance and medical attendance according to their means.

In January 1877 the special committee which had been formed to consider the new regulations concerning infectious diseases recommended that the new accommodation should be erected to the east of the existing buildings and in three separate blocks each capable of accommodating ten patients. The land on which the new wards were to be built belonged to the Marquess of Exeter and was valued at £540. The Marquess gave the amount of the purchase money as a donation to the new building. The three blocks were designed by Mr. Browning at a cost of £7,025. The buildings were opened in 1879. Following the original suggestion the three blocks were built to the east of the Infirmary with a space of between forty and fifty yards between each block. The blocks were each of two storeys with accommodation for five patients on each floor.

The planning of any additions to the original Infirmary had been given very little thought. The whole structure being more on the lines of a private house than a hospital. It would perhaps be fairer to say that the necessities of a hospital were not realised at that time. The comparison of Stamford Infirmary with others of similar date would certainly seem to suggest that architects of the day were content to use as their model the plan of an ordinary residence, making the easy working of the administration and the personal comfort of the permanent residents matters of paramount importance. Accommodation for an increasing number of patients (Stamford's population increased by 1,520 in the first twenty years of the Infirmary's existence) came as an after-thought.

Composite buildings such as the Infirmary, were open to contamination, not only from the patients but also from the kitchen odours and ill-placed sanitary arrangements. With new buildings being added to the original structure, the flow of air was gradually restricted until a situation was reached where the wards became unhealthy and caused additional medical problems. Such was the case at Stamford, and the situation was only relieved when air ducts were placed in the wards. It was further complicated by severe problems with sewerage. The original sewerage system was badly designed and a more complete system was installed. Unfortunately this system had no provision for preventing the return of sewer odours into the building, the result of which was to increase the amount of infection in the wards.

It is inevitable when tracing the history of an establishment such as the Infirmary that one comes across people who had devoted many years of their lives to the service of the institution. In this respect the service accorded to the Infirmary by the Hisset family is of particular interest. John Hisset, who came to Stamford from Kirby Underwood, was appointed to the position of porter on January 10th, 1837. His wife Abigail undertook the duties of laundress. During their time at the Infirmary, their two children were born, John in 1839 and Sarah in 1843. Of John we know very little other than the fact that he became a solicitor's clerk. Sarah on the other hand took up nursing and in 1869

15

at the age of 26 was appointed matron of the Infirmary where she had been born and where her father was still porter. She held this position until her retirement in 1904.

At the Annual Meeting of the Governors in January 1885, it was stated that the sum of £1,476 had been appropriated for extensive alterations due to the poor ventilation in the wards. Dr. Newman, surgeon to the Hospital, was not satisfied with the work, and the payment of the final instalment to the builders was withheld until "every part of the work was certified as satisfactory". The wisdom of this action by Dr. Newman became abundantly apparent when, five years later, the Recorder of Stamford said at the Quarter Sessions that "a serious epidemic had reached this country from Europe but was now largely on the wane, due to the excellent sanitary arrangements which had been obtained during the last five years and placed the population in such an advantageous position with regard to the epidemic".

During the later years of the century part of the Hospital's income was raised by the Saturday House to House Collection Fund (£376 in 1894), also by collections from the churches and chapels in the town and surrounding villages (£355 in 1895) as well as many gifts in kind such as flowers, fruit, vegetables, eggs and butter, especially at Harvest Festival time. This led to the establishment of a custom that the second or third Sunday in October should be called Hospital Sunday, on which every church donated its collections to the Infirmary.

In 1899 the total income from all sources was £2,234 (£2,290 in 1898) and expenditure £2,654 (£2,254) the latter being accounted for by the increased cost of provisions from £677 to £821, servants' wages including nurses from £441 to £588, and dressings and drugs from £190 to £234. But a greater number of infectious cases were treated, 57 against 40 in 1898, with an average stay in isolation of 54.3 days as compared with 34.2 the previous year. The longer time required for treatment was due to the increased number of cases of scarlet fever. The cost of maintenance of the Isolation Blocks had been met almost entirely from subsidies of £300 per annum from local Sanitary

Produced by J. E. C. Potter, from Photograph by Dr. Newman.

Produced by J. E. C. Potter, from Photograph by Dr. Newman.

1884

1928

1935

1942

1948

1968

1975

1978

Authorities. In a report published earlier in the year, Mr. Paget, the Medical Officer of Health for Northamptonshire County Council, when discussing "the measures which should be taken to prevent the spread of infectious diseases" stated that, "of the fever wards at Stamford Infirmary it is hardly possible to speak too highly. By a wise and generous policy the authorities have been led to open these wards to surrounding districts, which, thus fortunately placed, are excellently provided for".

On 3rd December 1903 Dr. William Newman died in the Stamford and Rutland Infirmary. He was born in Sheffield on 29th August 1833, the son of Robert Newman who was land agent to Earl Fitzwilliam at Wentworth Woodhouse in Yorkshire. After qualifying in medicine at St. Bartholomew's Hospital in London, he became an assistant to his uncle, Dr. Freeman Eaton at Ancaster, and later for a short time was in practice at Fulbeck in Lincolnshire, before moving to Stamford in 1862 where he was appointed surgeon to the Infirmary. By this time he had taken higher medical qualifications both as a physician and surgeon with the degrees of M.D. and M.R.C.P. (London) and F.R.C.S. (England). He had a large family practice in the town and villages around, as well as conducting a consultant practice which gave him the reputation of being one of the best known surgeons in the Midlands.

In 1863 he was offered the post of Assistant Physician at his old hospital but he preferred his country practice in Stamford, and remained there for the next forty years, thirty as surgeon and ten as consulting surgeon. Stamford Infirmary at that time had only thirty beds, most of which were filled with his patients.

He was a man of many interests, being a pioneer of sanitation and matters concerning public health, and he was also one of the first doctors to use X-rays for diagnostic purposes, at which he became an acknowledged expert. A man of unswerving integrity and utter loyalty, he was one of the great general practitioners of his time, a most excellent physician, a skilful and accomplished surgeon, but above all a practical man successful in curing his patients.

He finally retired to a lovely cottage in the village of Luffenham, but he was in failing health and gradually deteriorated until he could no longer be nursed at home and died in the hospital he loved so well.

On 21st July 1912 a Grand Pageant was held on the Infirmary lawn to represent and portray the visit to Stamford of Queen Elizabeth in 1565, when she dined at the Grey Friary as the guest of her Lord High Treasurer, William Cecil. She stayed the night at the Friary because serious illness prevalent at Burghley House prevented her from visiting it.

The principals in the pageant were mounted on horseback and all gaily costumed in accordance with the custom of the period. The procession assembled in the George Hotel yard and made its way to the Infirmary along streets lined by cheering crowds. On arrival, the pageant was enacted and included dances performed by local children to the accompaniment of a small orchestra directed by Mr. Malcolm Sargent A.R.C.O. The occasion resulted in a sum of £304.7.5d being donated towards the Infirmary funds.

The Part played by the Hospital in the Great War of 1914-18 was primarily to provide beds for wounded soldiers returning from France and Belgium, and yet at the same time to continue its services to the town and villages. It was supplemented by the provision of convalescent care at Burghley House, where the Marchioness of Exeter received the first 14 Belgian soldiers in December 1914. At the same time Lady Battie-Wrightson also opened her house at Wothorpe as a private auxiliary hospital with ten beds.

The following year an epidemic of diphtheria in the town severely strained the medical resources as well as draining the Town Council's coffers. The latter had an arrangement with the Hospital that for an annual retaining fee of £250 they could have the use of twenty beds in the Isolation Block, but any beds exceeding that number would be at the rate of six shillings per head per day. The epidemic cost the Council £500, the equivalent of a 3d rate.

18

The work of rehabilitating the wounded continued, and it was recorded at the Annual Meeting of Governors in January 1916 that there was a deficit of over £92 in the Accounts for the year, chiefly due to a rise of £300 in the cost of provisions and £150 in surgical requirements.

Entertainment for the soldiers in the form of concerts, dances and parties given by local dignitaries and tradesmen, did much to raise their morale after the atrocious conditions in the trenches. All this, however, was temporarily stopped by an edict from the Army Council in March 1917 that "there were to be no further tea parties as food is expensive and in short supply". Another way of showing their appreciation was soon found; it took the form of a Recreation Room erected on the front lawn of the Hospital, and generously donated by Mr. Stanley Brotherhood of Thornhaugh, a Governor of the Hospital. It measured 48 feet by 25 feet, and was familiarly known as the "New Hut"; it came into use in June 1917.

Seventeen months later the War was over, but the hut remained for some years as a token of those dark days.

In July 1920 the Army Council sent a Certificate to the Hospital expressing their thanks in the following terms:—

"During the Great War of 1914-19 this building was established and maintained as a Hospital for British sick and wounded; the Army Council in the name of the Nation thank those who have rendered to it this valuable and patriotic assistance in the hour of its emergency and they desire also to express their deep appreciation of the whole-hearted attention which the staff of this Hospital gave to the patients who were under their care; the War has once again called upon the devotion and self-sacrifice of British men and women and the Nation will remember with pride and gratitude their willing and inestimable service".

19

The Infirmary buildings and equipment had changed little over the past 96 years and were lamentably out of date. In May 1924 the Governors called a special meeting which was held in the Assembly Rooms, to launch an "Efficiency Fund" for a modernisation programme, in order to bring the Hospital up to "a standard to meet the requirements of the present day". This was to include the building of a Children's Ward (towards the cost of which £1,300 had already been donated from the balance of the Town War Memorial Fund) and a Maternity Ward, each with its own sun balcony. The treasurer of the Fund was Lord Exeter, and the target £12,000. A year later £3,700 had been donated by the public, and the building of the new wards was started at a cost of £8,000, the remaining £3,000 being provided by the Ministry of Health, thus enabling the building to be completed free of debt.

On 30th October 1926 H.R.H. the Princess Mary, only daughter of H.M. King George V, graciously performed the opening ceremony of the new Wing, of which the Children's Ward was in memory of those who fell in the Great War 1914-18. She was accompanied by her husband Viscount Lascelles, with whom in the presence of a distinguished gathering she inspected both wards, expressing delight at all she saw, especially the hand-painted friezes around the walls depicting well-known nursery rhymes. She made a complete tour of the Hospital and spoke to many of the patients. Lord Exeter's daughter, Lady Romayne Cecil had personally inaugurated an appeal to school children of the town a few weeks previously, to contribute to a Penny Fund to buy extra equipment for the Children's Ward, and she presented to Princess Mary a purse containing £150. The event was recorded by an inscribed plaque above a cot in the ward.

On the staff of the Hospital at this time was Dr. T. P. Greenwood, who in the following year completed 50 years of loyal and devoted service both as general practitioner and honorary surgeon to the Hospital, and for whom the public of Stamford showed their appreciation by subscribing to a fund which enabled his portrait to be painted; it hangs in the Consultant's Room to this day. His death occurred suddenly six months later.

1928 was Centenary Year, and in the 100th Annual Report on the state of the Stamford Rutland and General Infirmary, the Governors considered it to have been a highly satisfactory year, for the accounts showed a balance in hand of almost £200 on a turnover of £6,800. 713 patients were treated in the general wards, and out-patients numbered 1,345 with over 10,000 attendances: 401 operations were performed. The isolation wards in the Fever Blocks treated 49 cases of infectious illness, including 33 cases of scarlet fever, 11 of diphtheria and 5 of typhoid and paratyphoid fever. The income of the hospital was derived from many sources varying from annual subscriptions (£500) donations and legacies (£236) collections from places of worship (£243) collections from Stamford and surrounding villages, employees of firms in Stamford, and proceeds of whist drives (£1,110) payments by borough and county councils for infectious cases (£1,510) Infirmary Ball (£204) and even the sale of pigs (£59).

It is interesting to note that the Hospital was paying 1/- per lb for beef, 1/3d per lb for mutton, 7½d for a 4lb loaf of bread and 26/3d for a ton of best coal. The salary of the Matron was £120 per annum when Miss Elliott was appointed in 1930.

In June 1928 the Governors decreed that a committee should be appointed to prepare plans for proposed extensions and given authority to accept tenders not exceeding £14,000. At the same time the Trustees were instructed to sell some of their investments (which had a market value of over £19,000) to pay for the building as it proceeded.

It had long been the custom for sick people in the town who required treatment at the Hospital to be sponsored by a donor who could recommend as many patients as his donation warranted, either by direct admission or as an out-patient. In March 1931 a Contributory Scheme was launched covering the town and surrounding villages, with collectors in each, responsible for gathering in the weekly subscriptions, which would be 1d a week for wage earners between 14 and 18, and 2d a week for persons over 18 with an income not exceeding £5 a week. This entitled them to free treatment and maintenance if admitted to hospital for whatever reason.

The Scheme got off to a good start, but in June 1932 it became necessary to add an important rider to the conditions, namely "that all persons who have not joined or are in arrears with their subscription shall after 1st July pay full charges as fixed by the rules for in-patients, and to be fixed by the Weekly Board for out-patients. But such resolution is not to affect accidents, serious and urgent operations, or persons unable to pay through unemployment".

In December 1928 two private rooms were available in the Maternity Ward at a fee of £3. 3s. 0d per week, and in February 1930 the six private wards, built the previous year between the new male and female wards, were opened at a fee of £5. 5s. 0d per week.

In 1935 two well respected members of the medical staff retired, Lt-Col E. A. R. Newman, ophthalmic surgeon, and Mr. A. S. Jones, dental surgeon. Lt-Col Newman, son of a famous father Dr. William Newman, had embarked on a career in the Indian Medical Service where he served with distinction from 1893 until his retirement in 1926. He qualified at St. Bartholomew's Hospital, London in 1890, and had always been interested in ophthalmic surgery, so it was fitting that he should be the first holder of the appointment at Stamford. Mr. A. S. Jones had been honorary dental surgeon to the Hospital for the last 48 years and retired through ill health; his son, Gilbert, was immediately appointed to take his place. Both men were rewarded by being elected Life Vice-presidents of the Hospital.

Evidence of the uneasy state of Europe and of the war clouds looming ahead was shown by requests from Rutland County Council as early as October 1935, and Northamptonshire County Council in June 1937, for the provision of emergency beds in case of air raids. The

22

Managing Committee gave their consent "provided that accommodation is available when the event happens".

The general wards of the Hospital had been rebuilt and extended in 1929, but it was not until 1937 that the male and female wards were named Exeter and Ancaster respectively; at the same time the Children's Ward was named Princess Mary, with its side ward Newman; and the Maternity Ward was named Greenwood.

1938 was to go down in history as the year of Chamberlain and the Munich crisis, but for Stamford and Rutland General Infirmary it was a vitally important year as it presaged the beginning of a new era in the history of the Hospital. A small sub-committee of eight members of the Managing Committee had been appointed "to consider questions affecting the welfare and future well-being of the Infirmary". They had drawn up a suggested scheme for the reorganisation of Stamford Infirmary which included:

1. Finance. The previous year's accounts had shown a loss of £2,500. This was to be made good by increasing the Contributory Scheme charges by 1d in each category, which would supplement its income by £1,500. The remaining £1,000 to be raised by widening the Contributory Scheme to include persons whose incomes were greater than £250 p.a. by the payment of 6d per week, and to encourage payment by annual subscription.

2. Administration.
   (a) To appoint a full-time secretary at a salary of £450 p.a.
   (b) To replace the Weekly Board by a House Committee which would be responsible for the internal management of the Infirmary.
   (c) To increase the nursing staff, to enable them to work on the basis of a 96 hour fortnight.

It was unanimously agreed that these recommendations should be implemented on 1st January 1939. Mr. H. F. Donald was selected from an application list of 84 candidates to become the first secretary.

A SHORT HISTORY

With shorter working hours for nurses and no accommodation available for the extra number required (one sister and eight nurses), it was obvious that a new Nurses' Home was now a vital necessity. Plans were drawn up in July 1939 and in February 1940 the tender of Messrs Brick and Son for £7,210 was accepted: a year later it was opened without any fuss or ceremony. The war was now taking toll of many of the nursing and domestic staff who were being "called up" for other duties or transferred to other areas of the country; and this resultant shortage led to a low bed occupancy in the Hospital, despite the fact that many nurses were working up to 54 hours a week.

In January 1939 the last person was discharged from the Fever Blocks and they were closed until taken over in August as Casualty stations. The local A.R.P. Wardens started work at the outbreak of war and many times the Hospital was warned about lights showing in the black-out, and on more than one occasion was fined £5 for the offence.

Steel helmets, gas masks and stirrup-pumps were the order of the day and fire watching duties were organised on a voluntary basis.

Wothorpe House, situated on the southern edge of the town and owned by Lord Exeter, was taken over as an annexe to the Hospital for the care of forty convalescent and long-stay patients, having its own resident staff and sister-in-charge.

It was closed in August 1945. Meanwhile the Orangery at Burghley House had been converted in August 1944 to admit 25 convalescent patients. Between them these two annexes considerably relieved the pressure on the beds in the Hospital for more acute cases.

A very happy event in the annals of the Hospital took place on 12th June 1942 when Lady Exeter handed over to Lord Exeter, the Chairman of the Governors, a set of surgical and gynaecological instruments, valued at £170, from the Maple Leaf Fund of Pennsylvania U.S.A., together with a cheque for £250 from the Zonta Club of Canada in Toronto, for the purchase of a mobile X-Ray Unit; this was indeed a wonderful tribute from our Allies in America and Canada

24

at the time of this country's greatest need. This project had been arranged by Miss Daisy Bancroft, an American citizen, who, through friends in the district had been corresponding with Lady Exeter after she had seen an advertisement in a newspaper "for silk hose to be adapted for R.A.F. needs". From this came the idea of helping the Hospital by enlisting the aid of ten of her friends, who subscribed 850 dollars between them.

At the end of the ceremony the Chairman of the House Committee, Mr. C. H. Jones, gave Lady Exeter a penny as a token that no ill might come to either her Ladyship or the donors; this was later mounted and framed, the mount bearing an inscription commemorating the occasion. It now hangs in Matron's office. But this was not all, for in August there followed a gift of two 80 gallon drums of medicinal paraffin, enough to last the Hospital for the next two and half years.

The war dragged on and still the staffing difficulties continued, laundry workers and Irish maids leaving without warning, Sisters resigning for better jobs and eager probationers turned away because they were not capable of reaching the standards required for their initial training.

In February 1944 Mr. C. H. Jones died: he had served on most committees since 1930 and in view of his deep interest in the work of the Hospital and the great services he rendered, a bed was named in his memory in Exeter Ward. His successor as Chairman was Mr. F. W. C. Allen who continued in office until the inauguration of the National Health Service in 1948, when he was appointed Chairman of the Hospital Management Committee and a member of the Regional Board until the Reorganisation Scheme in 1974.

When the war in Europe ended on 8th May 1945, there was no holiday on this long awaited day for the hard worked hospital staff, simply because shortages in all the departments would not allow any absence from duty. But they had been working hard for the Hospital in other ways, for it is recorded on a plaque in the general office that "from August 1942 to May 1947 Stamford Infirmary Entertainments Committee raised £5,500 through Carnivals and other special efforts".

This was used to re-equip the X-Ray Department and provide £2,700 towards an extension to the Nurses' Home.

The end of the war brought with it further problems, for nationalisation of the Health Service was now becoming a distinct possibility, and Stamford's geographical position on the border of four counties meant that a choice had to be made between becoming part of the Sheffield Regional Board centred on that city 80 miles away to the north (by virtue of being in Lincolnshire), or alternatively of allying with Peterborough and thus becoming part of the East Anglian Regional Board with its headquarters at Cambridge 45 miles away to the south. The latter course was taken.

An outbreak of poliomyelitis in 1947 gave rise to much concern, and it was fortunate that the central Fever Block was available and ready for such cases; happily it also possessed an iron-lung machine which had been presented to all hospitals by Lord Nuffield at the beginning of the war, and this proved invaluable. Miss Mary Coyne was appointed Matron in May 1947; she had previously served as Sister in all departments of the Hospital during the early years of the war and left in 1941 to become Home Sister at Bury Infirmary. Her return as Matron was welcomed by all.

The year 1948 was probably the most important in the history of Stamford and Rutland General Hospital, for on 4th July it ceased to be a voluntary hospital under the control of its Governors and was incorporated in the state-controlled National Health Service under the Act of 1946.

Sadness was shared by all at the departure of the Marquess of Exeter, who had presided over the destinies of the Hospital since 1897, a record of service unsurpassed in the voluntary hospital movement. The Marchioness of Exeter had also been deeply involved during most of those 51 years as a member of Committee. At the final general meeting of the Contributory Scheme members, the Marquess thanked all those collectors and contributors who had helped to raise £100,000 for the

Hospital during the seventeen years since the Scheme was launched in 1931.

His last duty was to preside at the 119th and final meeting of the Board of Governors on 13th July 1948; in so doing he brought to a close one hundred and twenty years of continuous service as President of the Board by members of the Exeter family, starting with his great-grandfather the 2nd Marquess, and continued by his grand-father and father.

But the year brought some compensation to the nursing staff for all their trials and tribulations of the war years, by having a hard tennis court constructed for their use; and on the social side came the formation of a Branch of the Royal College of Nursing.

The House Committee ceased to exist on 4th July and was replaced by the Stamford and District Committee of the newly formed Hospital Management Committee, based on Peterborough at Group level and Cambridge at Regional Board level.

Changes in the Consultant staff followed thick and fast, but perhaps the biggest change was in the name of the Hospital, which in February 1949 became known as the Stamford and Rutland Hospital, having already dropped Infirmary from its title, and now no longer to be a General Hospital: it was at one time even suggested that it should be called by the impressive name of Stamford and Rutland Royal Hospital!

Once again accommodation for nurses was proving difficult to find as the new Home was full to capacity and the only long-term solution was to build a second storey above the existing building. Meanwhile, negotiations were taking place for the night nurses to be accommodated at Pilsgate House, a property owned by Lord Exeter about two miles from the Hospital, and it was ultimately agreed that it should be occupied in January 1949. The third Fever Block, still empty, was converted for domestic staff accommodation later in the year.

In 1957 the pattern of development was again changing, for in the twelve years since the war ended medical advances in treatment and technology revealed the urgent need for more sophisticated equipment and more space in which to house it. Extensions were necessary to the X-Ray, Physiotherapy and Out-patient/Casualty Departments; plans for a new centralised laundry were approved, but building did not start until the following year. The addition of a second storey to the Nurses' Home got underway in June 1956 and was completed early in 1957, thus allowing the use of Pilsgate House to be discontinued when the lease ran out in December 1956. Male and female Medical Wards were formed by the joining up of the ground floors of all three Fever Blocks, and constructing a covered way to link them with the main hospital. The pathology laboratory, created in 1951 in the third Fever Block, where it shared the ground floor with the occupational therapists, was in urgent need of more space and finally took over the floor above the medical wards.

Improved standards in Nursing Training meant that probationer nurses had to gain wider experience than could be offered at Stamford, and so a three month course in Psychiatry and Cardio-thoracic surgery at Rauceby and Papworth Hospitals respectively, was incorporated in the curriculum. As a result an annual recruitment of 18 to 20 girls could now complete their training with the approval of the General Nursing Council.

The Stamford Detachment of the British Red Cross set up a canteen in the Out-patients Department in November 1948 to supply snacks and hot drinks to patients awaiting appointments; ten years later their gifts to the hospital had amounted to £670, and their cheerful voluntary service played an integral part in relieving the anxiety of the visit to the doctor.

With an increasing number of consultants providing specialist care both in the wards and Out-patients, it now became necessary to find separate residential accommodation for more house doctors, and plans were drawn up for building new Quarters for them. These were eventually approved and work started in December 1963, but it was another year before the present Residency was ready for occupation.

Meanwhile, a new Staff dining room came into use in 1962, working on a cafeteria basis to feed all members of staff whatever their status in the Hospital.

Miss Coyne retired as Matron in November 1963 to return to her native Eire, having served the Hospital faithfully for 16 years, during which time she had steered it successfully through the difficult post-war period and the inception of the National Health Service. It is worthy of note that in 1967 the Hospital Social Club contributed £1,000 towards the construction of a Swimming Pool and £350 for a changing room. Four years later a Recreation Room was built next to the Staff Dining Room, and again the Social Club contributed one third of the total cost of over £2,500 in fulfilling a long-felt need for a place where nurses could relax or let off steam during off-duty periods.

The minutes of the Hospital Management Committee in January 1971 record the nuisance caused by pigeons at the front of the Hospital, and as permission to shoot them was not approved the matter was referred to the Local Authority, who suggested using traps, but as these were not successful their recommendation was to "trap those pigeons causing a nuisance".

The fuel crisis of 1972 caused the closure of Princess Mary and Greenwood Wards for three weeks during February and March; this high-lighted the growing concern over the low bed-occupancy of the former, which varied between 25% and 35% during the previous 12 months, for it was already being rumoured that the ward would be closing in the near future and all sick or injured children would be admitted to Peterborough District Hospital which had opened in 1968. A public meeting at the Town Hall in December 1974 unanimously opposed the closure but it was all to no avail, and Princess Mary Ward closed its doors as a Children's Ward on 19th November 1976.

The last meeting of the Stamford and District Committee of the Hospital Management Committee took place on 12th March 1974, and the implementation of the scheme for the Reorganisation of the National Health Service came into effect on 1st July 1974.

It was founded on a three-tier system of control, in which Stamford and Bourne formed an overlap area from Lincolnshire, to be administered by the Peterborough Health District, but only for hospital services. Peterborough and Cambridge Health Districts came under the control of the Cambridgeshire Area Health Authority (Teaching), and this body was finally responsible to the East Anglian Regional Health Authority in Cambridge.

This resulted in the winding up of the Hospital Management Committee, (which had been directly responsible to the old Regional Board), and being replaced by the District Management Team composed of six District Officers representing Administration, Community Health, Nursing, Finance, Consultants and General Practitioners.

For some time the surgical staff had been pressing for the up-grading of the operating theatre, which had been built in 1929 and was now rather out of date. The first plans were drawn up in January 1971 and the following year extra changing rooms and a central sterilising store were built on the west side of the theatre connected by a communicating corridor; this was only a temporary measure and proved to be uneconomic. And so in July 1973 plans for a new twin theatre complex were submitted, incorporating the latest modular design in which a steel hexagonal-shaped framework is fitted with an inner cladding. It was a completely self-contained unit with air conditioning, and supported by full ancillary services with anaesthetic and recovery rooms, rest rooms and changing rooms for the staff. Only one theatre was built, due to shortage of money, but all facilities were available for a second if the necessary funds were forthcoming in the future.

The old theatre was now converted for the use of the Medical Records Department which had previously been struggling to store an ever increasing number of records in accommodation much too small for its needs.

THE STAMFORD AND RUTLAND HOSPITAL

In 1977 Princess Mary Ward was taken over by the building contractors for conversion into a ten-bedded orthopaedic ward for adults; it reopened in September.

Day rooms were built on to the balconies of Ancaster and Exeter Wards and came into use in January 1978; they provide a comfortable place where convalescent patients can have a chat or watch television.

In conclusion, it must be mentioned that four members of the Hospital staff have each served in their respective offices for a period exceeding thirty years. Miss May Albon will complete forty years as secretary in the administrative office in May this year. She was awarded the Queen's Jubilee Medal in 1977: a well deserved honour for her long service to Stamford and Rutland Hospital. Sister Mary Coles has been nursing at the Hospital since she entered it as a probationer on 1st January 1944, becoming a staff nurse three years later, and for the last 27 years Sister of Exeter Ward.

Mr. George Tibbert has been employed in the kitchen since 1946. He started as a cook, soon became known as "chef" and in 1964 was promoted to Catering Manager. He now has charge of a much more modern kitchen than when he started. Thomas Simpson, to give him his full name, but more widely known as Tom, will complete thirty years service as gardener and general handyman in June this year.

THE FRIENDS OF THE STAMFORD HOSPITALS

Patrons:
The Most Hon. The Marquess of Exeter, K.C.M.G.
The Right Hon. The Earl of Ancaster, K.C.V.O.

Treasurer:	Chairman:	Secretary:
Cdr. L. Lumley,	J. R. Thompson, Esq.,	H. E. Packer, Esq.,
Church Cottage,	Collyweston House,	'Holwell',
Mill Street,	Collyweston,	St. Paul's Street,
Duddington, Stamford.	Nr. Stamford.	Stamford.
Tel: Duddington 280	Tel: Duddington 275	Tel: Stamford 3455

General Committee

Mrs. J. M. Holt, Vice Chairman
Mr. T. G. Clancy
Mr. A. M. Govey
Mr. H. S. Scorer
Mrs. M. Bradshaw
Mrs. A. Lumley
Mrs. M. Atkins
Mrs. J. Cross
Mr. R. Oak
Mr. D. Cross
Lady Jane Willoughby
Miss M. Bauld, Matron
Mr. D. V. Clarke, Hospital Secretary

FRIENDS OF THE STAMFORD HOSPITALS

At a Public Meeting in the Town Hall on 11th October 1962, at which the Mayor, Alderman A. S. Ireson presided, it was decided to form the Friends of the Stamford Hospitals, a charitable organisation affiliated to the National Society of Friends.

Dr. J. A. Dale was elected the first Chairman.

Not until December 1963, when it became registered as a charity, did it really embark on its main task "to provide amenities and comforts for the patients and staff" not covered by the Health Service.

Its first job was to provide furniture for the mortuary and to ensure that fresh flowers were placed on the altar each week: this custom has continued.

In the early days the Stamford Round Table figured prominently in raising money for the Friends, besides organising a car service for relatives unable to visit the Hospital on account of transport difficulties. In March 1966 Dr. Dale died soon after returning from a holiday in New Zealand; a Memorial Garden was created in his memory in the Hospital grounds. In his place Mr. J. R. Thompson was elected Chairman and Mrs. J. M. Holt Vice Chairman, and these two hold office today.

Summer fetes have been held on the Hospital lawns in alternate years since 1965 and raised over £6,000; the highlight of these was in 1971 when the fete was opened by Mr. Ernie Wise, and for the first time over £1,000 was raised by the Friends for their funds. Mr. Ron Oak has organised a Grand Raffle every Christmas and raised over £2,200 in the last nine years.

Donations by the Friends include such diverse gifts as curtains for all wards, eight ripple beds, six King Edward Fund beds, an incubator and obstetric table for the Maternity Ward, Bleep System for the staff, television sets for the Nurses' Home and the wards, Summer House for St. George's Hospital, annual fireworks for the children on

33

Guy Fawkes night, a special examination lamp for Casualty, and their biggest project of all, "Operation Facelift" for the Casualty/Out-patient waiting area, which transformed a 19th Century building into a modern, bright and colourful department.

In the Autumn of 1977 a magnolia tree was planted to celebrate the Silver Jubilee of Her Majesty the Queen, and in December a Phototherapy Unit was presented to the Maternity Ward for the treatment of babies with jaundice.

To mark the 150th Anniversary, a Fayre is being held in the Hospital grounds on Saturday 10th June 1978.

All proceeds from the sale of this book will be donated to The Friends of the Stamford Hospitals.

MATRONS AT
STAMFORD AND RUTLAND GENERAL INFIRMARY

1827 — 1831   Miss Susanna Clarke
1831 — 1859   Miss Eliza Simpson
1859 — 1869   Miss Eliza Lovell   *Died in 1869*
1869 — 1904   Miss Sarah Hissett
1904 — 1906   Miss Vaughan
1906 — 1913   Miss Browne
1913 — 1915   Miss Jones
1915 — 1917   Miss Leah Morris
1917 — 1928   Miss Marie Goodrich
1928 — 1930   Miss A. W. Willis
1930 — 1945   Miss I. Elliott
1945 — 1947   Miss K. Grayson
1947 — 1963   Miss Mary Coyne
1963 — 1965   Miss E. M. Smart
1966 — 1967   Miss Joan Palmer *(Acting Matron)*
1967 —   Miss Mary Bauld

SECRETARIES AT STAMFORD AND RUTLAND HOSPITAL

1939 — 1958   Mr. H. F. Donald
1958 — 1964   Mr. J. A. Trevor
1964 — 1966   Mr. H. J. Richards
1966 — 1968   Mr. E. Smith
1968 — 1971   Mr. W. J. Mortlock
1971 —   Mr. D. V. Clarke

THE CONTINUING STORY
1978 TO 2015

Henry Friar: the original benefactor of Stamford Hospital.

With grateful thanks to Chris Davies for his very substantial contribution to writing much of this recent history and also to his considerable involvement in the production of the history written in 1978. We are also grateful to many others, particularly Gillian Langley and David Baxter.

By the time Stamford Hospital celebrated 150 years in 1978, the National Health Service itself had reached its 30th birthday. At the time that the first part of the Hospital's story was drawn to a close the seeds of change, both in management strategy and clinical advances, had already been sown in the NHS and health care. To some extent the NHS had become a victim of its own success and changes were taking place nationally which would have significant effects on Stamford Hospital. Many years previously Aneurin Bevan had said of the NHS "the service must always be growing, changing and improving". This was most certainly to be the case. The introduction of modem imaging and minimal access surgical techniques are just two examples in the ongoing evolution of medical practices which were to bring about change in the way patients received treatment.

Nationally, as well as locally, more people were being treated in increasingly complex ways. In general, this led to greater expectations of the health service, particularly in an increasingly elderly population. The next thirty years would see even greater changes in the way that healthcare was perceived, with the 'patient' being seen as a customer of hospital services, with very specific rights under Patient Charters.

Stamford Hospital's ability to meet these changing needs was one of mixed fortunes. While the Hospital continued to develop and do excellent work, developments over the next 37 years were to see a gradual reduction in the levels of in-patient service the Hospital was called upon to provide. In 1978 Stamford Hospital continued as part of the Peterborough Health District with Consultant Medical Staff being drawn from Peterborough. Some outpatient clinics were based in prefabricated buildings which had been brought over from Peterborough in 1968. While it was recognised in a Health Authority report of 1980 that these needed replacing, another decade was to pass before this actually came to fruition. The same report saw the need for a second theatre but, in the event, this was not approved. The report also considered that the pharmacy accommodation was inadequate, although the service provided was good. Throughout the 1980s and 1990s the Hospital pharmacy was a very busy department. In addition to supplying medication to in-patients and outpatients at Stamford Hospital, it also provided a service to Bourne, the Gloucester Centre in Peterborough and Doddington Hospital.

Stamford Hospital: 1988

For the architects of public services in the 1980s and 1990s the cri de coeur was 'centralisation' with bigger acute hospitals serving larger areas. In a consultation paper published in 1980, Gerard Vaughan, the then Minister of Health, drew attention to the trend for larger hospitals; some of those being planned were very large indeed with 1,000 beds or more. While rehearsing the medical and financial advantages of larger hospitals, the Minister was also mindful that there was a real risk of concentrating services more heavily than the advantages justified, to the detriment of such things as the accessibility of hospitals to both patients and visitors, and the sense of identity which many communities have with their local hospital – an argument that was to be put forward many times in the coming years by the people of Stamford. The paper also drew attention, not that it was needed, to the fact that there was a finite amount of money in the NHS pot, and the building of larger hospitals would inevitably mean the closure of some smaller local hospitals.

Given the small size of Stamford Hospital, it is easy to forget that it was always very busy. With advances in anaesthesia and surgical techniques, more complex operations could be undertaken in Stamford. During the 1980s hip and knee replacements, as well as major gynaecological and urological procedures became routine. All ten theatre sessions were fully utilised for general surgery, gynaecology, urology, ENT and orthopaedics with the procedures being carried out by consultant surgeons and anaesthetists from Peterborough District Hospital.

In 1984 2,300 operations were performed at Stamford, the highest number in any theatre in the Peterborough Health District. Ten years later, in 1994, this number had risen to 2,575.

The concept of a large district hospital in Peterborough did not sit well with the people of Stamford, who had grown much attached to their local hospital and, whenever possible, they would always opt to go the Stamford Hospital rather than travel to Peterborough. The closure of Princess Mary childrens' ward in 1976 was something of a blow, which had not been well received locally. However, the opening of Peterborough District Hospital in 1968 saw the beginning of a gradual shift in medical services from Stamford to Peterborough. The decision in December 1988 to transfer maternity services to Peterborough was to see the first public demonstration by the people of Stamford against moving services from Stamford to Peterborough. For many, the closure of Princess Mary and Greenwood wards seemed to signal the complete closure of the Hospital.

Despite all this, the interest that local people had in their Hospital did not diminish. In June 1995, the Hospital staged its first ever 'Open Evening', which was organised by Gill Langley. The event attracted over 300 visitors, who were able to see most areas of the Hospital including the operating theatre, casualty, out-patients, pathology and physiotherapy. Hospital staff were kept very busy all evening answering the many questions posed by interested visitors.

The role of Stamford hospital in training nurses is another aspect of hospital life that should not be overlooked. Although training for State Registered Nurses (SRN) had ceased by 1974, the two year programme for 40 State Enrolled Nurses (SEN) continued until 1983. The pupil nurses were resident in the Nurses' Home on the hospital site and undertook their theoretical training at the Peterborough School of Nursing. The practical elements of their training and on-going assessment were undertaken on the wards and departments at Stamford.

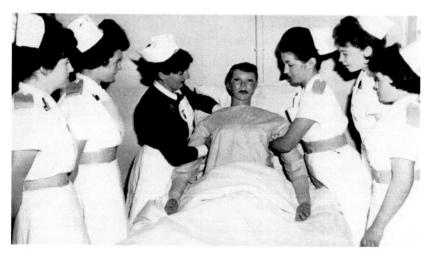

In the practical classroom

An interesting reminder of the earlier days of the hospital surfaced (quite literally) in 1983. During routine maintenance and decorating, a number of tile pictures were uncovered in Hurst ward. Research in the Hospital archives showed that they were an integral part of the wall structure, and had cost £75.1s.3d. when the building was constructed in 1878. Further investigation discovered that there were 18 in all, situated in the Clay, Hurst and Cecil blocks. Experts from the Tile Museum at Telford confirmed that they were of national interest, and probably manufactured by Minton.

Fever Block Tile Picture: 1878

The intervention of successive governments in the management of the NHS is an interesting study in its own right. However, for the purpose of this history, we need only look at those changes that had a significant effect on Stamford Hospital. In 1983, Margaret Thatcher had commissioned Sir Ernest Griffiths to produce a report on the management of the NHS. This report, amongst other things, led directly to the introduction of General Management in the NHS. This was not a move that was generally welcomed, and many doctors and nurses feared that their professions would lose influence after the dissolution of consensus management teams. The RCN mounted a vigorous campaign against the move.

However, a general management system was introduced. In August 1986 the two posts of Director of Nursing and Administrative Manager were combined to produce the new post of General Manager. The first holder of the new post at Stamford was Gill Langley, who had first joined the hospital in 1980 as Senior Nursing Officer before becoming Director of Nursing Services in 1982.

Despite the prevailing feeling that the hospital might be closing, there was still much happening that gave cause for optimism. With the creation of an internal market in the NHS reforms, Stamford Hospital was managerially separate from Peterborough, and was assessed as a standalone unit. It was probably because of this, that there had been little capital investment for a considerable period of time. However, all of this was about to change. The North West Anglia Healthcare Trust (of which Stamford was part) agreed to fund the building of a new Outpatients Department from its Treasury capital monies. Early in 1988, a donation of £1.1 million by the Van Geest family allowed the development of a new geriatric unit to replace the old St George's Hospital.

Mr and Mrs Van Geest at sod turning, August 26th 1988

The John Van Geest unit was opened in 1989 with a total of 24 beds; 20 single rooms and 2 doubles. The new Casualty, Outpatients, Radiology, Pharmacy, Medical Records, New Day Hospital and Physiotherapy departments were opened in 1989. The transfer of most of the departments from the old to the new in the space of one weekend was achieved with assistance of family and friends, young and old. Gill Langley writing in the Trust's in-house journal Update said:

"One of our greatest achievements and an indicator of the tremendous spirit amongst the staff was the move from the old Casualty/OPD to the new building over a single weekend. Departments closed at 5pm on Friday and reopened at 9am on Monday in totally new surroundings. Patient care was not interrupted for a single hour". Given that the charitable nature of healthcare was largely a thing of the past with the inception of the NHS, it is interesting to record that the new geriatric unit was brought about by a charitable donation and not NHS funding.

The Duchess of Gloucester opening the X-ray department: September 11th, 1990

In 1992, £537,000 was set aside for a complete modernisation and expansion of the kitchens. This was in addition to the £4 million that had been invested in the hospital in the previous four years. The number of patients seen by the hospital was steadily increasing, and in 1994 it carried out:

32,169	*pathology tests*
19,870	*outpatient appointments*
13,116	*x-rays*
7,404	*physiotherapy appointments*
6,500	*casualty cases*
2,575	*operations*

It is perhaps worth noting here, that while we might regret the closing of surgical wards, the fact remains that with the advances in medical practice, it was now possible to treat many more people as day cases. While in some cases this might entail an overnight stay in the hospital, the majority of patients were discharged to their home on the same day.

The necessary upgrade of the kitchen reminds us that hospitals need ancillary services in order to complete their primary task of healthcare. The catering department at Stamford Hospital was a considerable operation in its own right. During an average day the department produced nearly 300 meals for inpatients and 20 for day patients in addition to the meals for the staff dining room which was a popular facility much appreciated by all hospital staff. The catering department also produced 400 meals monthly for Lincolnshire CC day hospital; and for Meals on Wheels they produced over 800 meals per week. If that were not enough, they also had a contract to supply meals for prisoners at Stamford Police Station. Another very busy department was the Hospital laundry which had been opened in 1959. This department gave sterling service and provided laundry services for most of the other hospitals in the area including Peterborough, Doddington, Wisbech and Kings Lynn. However, changes in the structure of the management between Peterborough and Stamford hospitals resulted in the decision by Peterborough not to renew its contract with Stamford hospital laundry. This decision rendered the unit financially unviable and so, after 35 years, the laundry closed in 1994 with the loss of 41 staff.

Group Laundry, Stamford Hospital. 1998

With the demise of the laundry, the steam heating system for the whole site from a coal fired boiler became uneconomic and the hospital areas were converted to individual gas heaters. This freed the whole laundry/ boilerhouse area for development and it was sold with the staff swimming pool and unused doctors' residence to the Sheepmarket Surgery for a new surgery with Coop Pharmacy. (2000)

Although hospitals are primarily about their patients, they are also a community in their own right, and communities do things together. There is a long tradition at the hospital for staff get-togethers and joint activities. In 1978, the Hospital Quiz was started to celebrate the 150th anniversary. This consisted of teams of 4 (usually including a consultant) from most of the wards and departments all vying to show their knowledge. The quiz has continued to the present day, although the teams now are open to friends and families. The biennial fete, a feature of pre-NHS fund raising, which was restarted in 1965, was another occasion which brought the hospital staff together in a major fundraising event for the Friends of Stamford Hospital, and continued until the early 1990's.

At the dawn of the new millennium, Stamford Hospital still faced an uncertain future. Stamford remained part of the Northwest Anglia Healthcare Trust which had been formed in 1993. However, a mere nine years later in 2002, the Trust was disbanded and Stamford became part of the Peterborough Hospitals NHS Trust. In 2003 the Peterborough & Stamford Hospitals NHS Foundation Trust was formed and became operative from 1st April 2004. This was one of the first ten foundation trusts created under the NHS Act 2003. NHS Foundation Trusts were designed as independent legal entities with unique governance arrangements and accountable to local people, who could become members and governors. Each NHS Foundation Trust has a duty to consult and involve a board of governors (including patients, staff, members of the public and partner organisations) in the strategic planning of the organisation.

Prior to Stamford Hospital joining the Peterborough Hospitals NHS Trust, there was a multi-million pound plan to improve services and facilities. This plan was taken forward as the Stamford Hospital Investment Plan (SHIP) with three sub groups looking at clinical strategy, project planning and workforce planning. The intention was that the groups would redevelop the original plans, whilst ensuring they complemented the Greater Peterborough health investment plan. An event was held at the Stamford Arts Centre on 9th December 2003 to present the plans to the public.

Concerns about the hospital were however, never very far from the surface. In March 2005 the Chief Executive Officer moved to refute rumours that there were plans to close Stamford Hospital. This followed the disclosure that the hospital site had been put forward by SKDC for potential redevelopment. SKDC documents suggested that the site had the potential for 30 houses. This fuelled the growing public fear that, with the development of the new Peterborough City Hospital, Stamford Hospital would be phased out.

On 14 June 2005 the Chief Executive explained the Trust's strategy to Stamford Town Council. The council asked for guarantees that Stamford Hospital would remain open; while the CEO confirmed that there was no intention to close the hospital he continued by saying that 'nothing was guaranteed in the NHS and things seldom stay the same for long'. This was cold comfort for those concerned for the future of the hospital.

Since 2002, Stamford had experienced a number of cuts to wards and services with the closure of the Exeter ward for surgical patients in 2004 followed by the Hurst ward's medical and rehabilitation beds in 2005. This latter closure came only a short while after the reassurances given by the CEO. While some ward closures can be said to have been medically driven, this was not the case with the closure of Hurst ward, which was done without consultation, and was clearly financially driven. The closure of Hurst ward again raised a storm of protest, and saw many local people joining a protest march through the streets of the town.

Protest March through Stamford: July, 2005

In April 2010 P&SHT announced that Stamford Hospital was to undergo a £12m revamp with the development of a health campus. A spokesperson at that time said that this would be the 'biggest development in healthcare in Stamford for many years'. Future events however, were to see the £12m figure reduced considerably. Financial issues again came to fore in June 2011, when the P&SHT announced it was looking to lose some 300 staff in order to plug a £38m deficit in its budget.

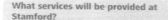

What services will be provided at Stamford?

The Trust has already made a commitment to retain the mobile MRI scanner and has invested more than £250,000 in digital x-ray services. On top of this, we have also transferred services such as pain management, haematology and oncology to Stamford. As well as this, we think there is scope for reintroducing a range of antenatal services, carrying out renal dialysis and chemotherapy, and completing more day surgery and outpatient care. Of course, all of this will be discussed with GPs who will need to commission these services from us if we provide them at Stamford.

How long is the redevelopment scheduled to take?

Planning processes can be uncertain, however we anticipate that planning will take place throughout 2011 and building will be completed by the end of 2013. As we redevelop the site, we can begin to introduce some of the service improvements as we go along.

Who are the technical advisors and what do they do?

Our technical advisors for the project comprise WSP, Devereux architects, WT partnership health planners and construction cost consultants, David Langdon. We have first hand experience of WSP as they were also technical advisors for Peterborough City Hospital. We know they have wide experience of working in the NHS and they have specific experience of working with historic buildings. We need technical advisors to help us with additional skills we would not normally expect to have in house, but they very much work as part of our single team.

Will the site be demolished?

Over the years the site at Stamford has changed, and we need to make some considerable changes to ensure that the quality of care and facilities we provide there continue to be of the highest possible standard. Not all of the existing buildings are suitable for redevelopment and we are currently working to identify these areas. Some other areas may be more suitable for a different use and, again, we are identifying those at the moment.

What will happen to the listed buildings?

We are aware that there are some listed buildings on the site and we will be working through our planning advisors with the Civic Society and English Heritage.

Will parts of the site be sold?

This depends a great deal on partners such as how GPs, social services and voluntary organisations want to work with us to develop a health campus. However, like all public sector organisations we are looking at innovative ways of funding projects such as this redevelopment. We may well want to work with third parties to enable us to invest in the provision of key facilities such as a state of the art day surgery unit and theatre suite.

What will you do about car parking?

We want more people to use Stamford Hospital and clearly parking is a major consideration for our patients and our staff. When we submit a planning application we will need to include a travel plan, but work on this has not yet started.

Peterborough and Stamford Hospitals Foundation Trust leaflet outlining plans [unfulfilled] for redevelopment: 2010

The spectre of closure arose again in 2012/13 hard on the heels of the financial problems experienced by the new Peterborough City Hospital. The PFI-funded Peterborough Hospital had entered a high profile financial melt-down, and the accountants were necessarily looking to see where money could be saved. Concerns for Stamford were heightened further when it was announced that the Pathology Department would relocate to Peterborough at the end of August 2012.

The Van Geest unit no longer had 24-hour medical cover, which meant that Greenwood ward, providing day surgery, could no longer keep patients in overnight if they were slow to recover. Out of hours GP services, which for a time were located at the hospital were also moved elsewhere. All of this, together with earlier ward closures, had resulted in a seriously under-used site, a factor which was to prove crucial to the future development plans for Stamford. In addition to this, the hospital also faced moves to axe much of the remaining day surgery services, with plans to end operations under general anaesthetic, which would be moved to Peterborough.

Stamford Hospital's unenviable position in relation to the financial problems of Peterborough City Hospital eventually caught the eye of the national press, and a number of newspapers commented on it. Although not typical, the satirical magazine Private Eye in February 2013 referred to the slow demise of Stamford Hospital.

In March 2013 the CEO addressed Stamford Town Council and assured them that there was every intention of keeping Stamford Hospital open. He told councillors that plans to spend £3.8 million over three years in redeveloping the hospital were still on the table. However, he went on to say that it would be inappropriate to take the business case any further while the Contingency Planning Team was looking at options across the wider health economy. It was also stressed that the options of selling part of the site, or closing Stamford Hospital, were still there. In September 2012 it had been proposed that 60% of the site could be sold off to not-for-profit partners to develop the site as a healthcare campus. The Stamford MP Nick Boles expressed fears that the cash crises faced by the Peterborough and Stamford NHS Hospitals Trust would mean that the plans to re-vamp the site into a healthcare campus would be shelved. Mr Boles suggested that if the Trust could not carry out its plans, then another Trust should consider taking on Stamford.

Despite years of uncertainty about the Hospital's future, there is still room for optimism. In September 2013, following considerable work by the Contingency Planning Team, the sector Regulator for Health Services (Monitor) issued its report on the options for the Peterborough and Stamford Hospitals NHS Trust. In the report Monitor authorised the Trust to make its own decisions on the proposed redevelopment of Stamford Hospital, stating that it (Monitor) agreed with the recommendation of the Contingency Planning Team that the Hospital should be considered an integral part of the Trust's future services and clinical strategy.

At a meeting on 24th September 2013, the Trust Board agreed to support the recommendation to redevelop the Hospital at a gross cost of £3.8 million over a three year period. The option of marketing that part of the site which had been earmarked for lease or sale was to be considered by the Board by the end of March 2014. The Trust Board's decision in relation to the Stamford and Rutland Hospital Redevelopment Project was referred to the Council of Governors, and received ratification on 9th October 2013.

Nursing staff on the Day Case Unit on Greenwood Ward, 2014

At the end of 2014, Stamford Hospital had already provided 186 years of unbroken service to the people of Stamford and surrounding area.. The nature of the care provided however, had changed. Advances in medicine, clinical practice and surgery, undreamt of in Henry Fryer's day, means that there is now much less reliance on long stays in hospital; many procedures that, even a few years ago, would have required a stay in hospital, can now be undertaken in a day and the patient discharged home to recuperate. Any doubts about Stamford's importance as a community hospital are soon dispelled when we look the work being undertaken there. The total number of patients treated in 2013 and 2014 show a steady increase, and it would be reasonable to expect this trend to continue.

	2013	2014
Outpatients	37408	39270
John Van Geest	486	443
Minor Injuries Unit	8544	8921
Day Surgery Unit	3877	3241
X-ray	18567	19644
Phlebotomy	28135	28058
Therapy Services	8236	7519

The future therefore seems positive. After many years of concern there now seems a firm commitment to include Stamford Hospital as an integral part of the Peterborough and Stamford Hospitals NHS Foundation Trust's future development. Patient numbers have progressively increased over the years, with some 107,096 patients being seen in 2014. While part of the site will be sold off, new developments which will include additional outpatients' facilities, two procedure rooms and an MRI scanner are a significant step forward. The notion of developing a healthcare campus on that part of the site not currently used, has much to commend it, and is surely one that Henry Fryer himself would have approved.

Stamford Hospital has always been popular with patients and staff. There are many reasons for this but perhaps the high quality of its staff has been a key factor in its success.

Nurses' Day at Stamford Hospital; 2015

THE FRIENDS OF STAMFORD HOSPITAL

The Friends of the Stamford Hospitals was established following a public meeting in the Town Hall of Stamford on October 11th 1962. It was not though until December 1963 that it was registered as a charity and started to undertake its main task of providing amenities and comforts for the patients and staff of the Hospital. At this time the NHS was only 15 years old and there were still many gaps in what was available to make the Hospital more comfortable for patients.

The objects of the Friends are listed in the Constitution, and remain as relevant in 2015 as they did in 1963. In particular, the Friends work hard to foster and reflect the support of local people in the work of the Hospital, for example by encouraging membership, providing regular information and holding meetings. They are also active in raising funds that have been used for a wide variety of purposes and increasingly to fund extra pieces of equipment to help develop further the services offered at the Hospital.

The patrons of the Friends in 1963 were the Marquess of Exeter and the Earl of Ancaster, and their successors have kindly agreed to continue this role, the patrons in 2015 being Miranda Rock and Lady Jane Willoughby.

50th Anniversary of the Friends: 2013

The committee of the Friends meets four times a year to discuss fund raising, to receive requests for funding and discuss any other issues affecting the Hospital. The current Matron, Susan Brooks, attends these meetings and gives invaluable advice about services that deserve support, and often other members of staff attend to make their case.

Chairmen of the Friends
1963 - 1966 Dr Dale
1966 - 1979 Mr R Thompson
1979 - 1994 Mr D Felton
1994 - present date Dr M W Dronfield

Secretaries
1963 - 1989 Mr W Packer
1989 - 1995 Mrs R Burt
1995 - 1999 Mrs K Hircock
1999 - 2003 Mr D Baxter
2003 - 2011 Mr J Hale
2011 - present date Mrs K Hircock

Treasurers
Cdr L Lumley; Mr K Bannister; Mr J Scholes

Annual Bill Packer Lecture
Bill Packer was Secretary of the Friends at the start and remained so for 26 years. He made a great contribution to the establishment and subsequent success of the Friends, and after his death in 1994 an annual memorial lecture in his name was established. Many of the lecturers have been Old Stamfordians [OS] who were at Stamford School when Bill taught there.

The lecturers have been
1995:   MJKSmith [OS]. Previous Captain of the England cricket team.
1996:   Dr Eric Till. Retired Stamford GP and local historian.
1997:   Philip Goodrich [OS]. Bishop of Worcester. "Making sense of the Present".
1998:   Geoffrey Timm. Headmaster Stamford School.
1999:   Lady Victoria Leatham. Patron of the Friends. "Burghley House".

2000: Baroness Willoughby de Eresby. Patron of the Friends. "Primary healthcare in Jordan's desert".

2001: Dr M MacGregor. Bourne GP."The Canals of Britain".

2002: Major General John Drewienkiewicz [OS]. Senior army officer.

2003: Chris Catlin [OS]. "A Newsman's view of the World"

2004: Peter Fraser. Headmaster Stamford School. "Education: is it wasted on the young?"

2005: Alan Maddox [OS]. "Policing London- Service and Education".

2006: David Baxter. Pathology Manager, Stamford Hospital. "The History of Stamford Hospital".

2007: Squadron Leader Al Pinner [OS]. "The Battle of Britain Memorial Flight: Fifty Years of the Men in Black".

2008: Simon Sharp. Previous Teacher at Stamford School. "Leonardo: a genius or just well educated?"

2009: Kathy Joyce and David Lankester. "Working, wandering and wondering: VSO in the Gambia and Pakistan".

2010: Paul Chirico [OS]. "The poetry of John Clare".

2011: Pat King [OS]. "The Falklands War: Overview of the RAF involvement before and after".

2012: Robert Forrest [OS]. "Hair strand testing: the Emperor's new wig?"

2013: Will Phelan. Headmaster Stamford School. "History and Characters of Stamford School".

2014: Miranda Rock. "Burghley: the last 30 years".

2015: Carl Killgren. "Economics is really VERY interesting".

The Volunteers:

The volunteers working in the Hospital are affiliated to the Friends and all are honorary members. They play an important role in guiding patients when they arrive at the Hospital, and by providing a friendly and helpful welcome. They also sell second hand books, raising several thousand pounds annually for the Friends.

Hospital Volunteers Training Day: 2011

Friends' Events

The biennial Hospital fete started in 1965 and continued until the early 1990's. In its heyday it attracted large crowds and a useful income for the Friends, but attendance fell away as such fetes became less popular. We still arrange and support fund raising events where we can. We have an annual Christmas quiz in the Hospital which was established in 1978 and has proven very popular over the years. At our AGM we always have a medical speaker, usually a local consultant who does sessions at the Hospital, and the annual Bill Packer lecture draws a good turnout.

Financial support

The income of the Friends comes from a variety of sources. Many people like to give to a local charity and this is very evident by the generous bequests we receive. We are supported by various charitable events such as the annual Santa Fun Run, and by sponsored events such as the Three Peaks Challenge. Book sales in the Out Patient department raise close to

£4000 annually, a considerable achievement at 50p per book.

Our income varies from year to year and is usually £15-20,000. We publish on our website the details of the projects we support. A considerable sum is spent on medical equipment such as a visual field analyser, hysteroscopes, bladder scanner, colonoscope and specialist surgical instruments. We are always pleased to provide funds for equipment that will improve patient comfort such as gynaecological couches and reclining chairs. We have also refurbished rooms such as creating an ophthalmology examination room, a dispensing area on the ward and relatives' room.

Stamford Hospital Museum

David Baxter delivering a talk on the History of the Hospital in the Museum: November, 2013

Many fascinating documents and ancient items of equipment have been stored at the Hospital over its long history and were in danger of being lost. At the initiative of Susan Brooks, the Matron, and supported by a hard working and enthusiastic committee of staff and local people, the Hospital Museum was established in 2010. It is currently sited in an empty bay on Hurst Ward on the ground floor of one of the fever blocks. There have been many visitors over the last 5 years and great interest has been shown in the contents. The Friends have made significant financial contributions to the Museum to help ensure its success.

Stamford Hospital Museum opening: August 6th, 2010

Influencing the future

There is strong local support for the Hospital and we articulate that whenever we can, for example at the regular Stamford Hospital Development Advisory Committee and the Stamford Town Council Health Committee.

*Further information including details on how to become a member can be found on our website: **www.friendsofstamfordhospital.org.uk** Selection*